New Directions for
Higher Education

Betsy O. Barefoot
Jillian L. Kinzie
CO-EDITORS

Intellectual Property, Faculty Rights and The Public Good

Samantha
Bernstein-Sierra
Adrianna Kezar
EDITORS

Number 177 • Spring 2017
Jossey-Bass
San Francisco

Intellectual Property, Faculty Rights and The Public Good
Samantha Bernstein-Sierra and Adrianna Kezar
New Directions for Higher Education, no. 177
Co-editors: *Betsy O. Barefoot and Jillian L. Kinzie*

NEW DIRECTIONS FOR HIGHER EDUCATION, (Print ISSN: 0271-0560; Online ISSN: 1536-0741), is published quarterly by Wiley Subscription Services, Inc., a Wiley Company, 111 River St., Hoboken, NJ 07030-5774 USA.

Postmaster: Send all address changes to NEW DIRECTIONS FOR HIGHER EDUCATION, John Wiley & Sons Inc., C/O The Sheridan Press, PO Box 465, Hanover, PA 17331 USA.

Information for subscribers
New Directions for Higher Education is published in 4 issues per year. Institutional subscription prices for 2017 are:
Print & Online: US$454 (US), US$507 (Canada & Mexico), US$554 (Rest of World), €363 (Europe), £285 (UK). Prices are exclusive of tax. Asia-Pacific GST, Canadian GST/HST and European VAT will be applied at the appropriate rates. For more information on current tax rates, please go to www.wileyonlinelibrary.com/tax-vat. The price includes online access to the current and all online backfiles to January 1st 2013, where available. For other pricing options, including access information and terms and conditions, please visit www.wileyonlinelibrary.com/access.

Delivery Terms and Legal Title
Where the subscription price includes print issues and delivery is to the recipient's address, delivery terms are **Delivered at Place (DAP)**; the recipient is responsible for paying any import duty or taxes. Title to all issues transfers FOB our shipping point, freight prepaid. We will endeavour to fulfil claims for missing or damaged copies within six months of publication, within our reasonable discretion and subject to availability.

Back issues: Single issues from current and recent volumes are available at the current single issue price from cs-journals@wiley.com.

Disclaimer
The Publisher and Editors cannot be held responsible for errors or any consequences arising from the use of information contained in this journal; the views and opinions expressed do not necessarily reflect those of the Publisher and Editors, neither does the publication of advertisements constitute any endorsement by the Publisher and Editors of the products advertised.

Publisher: New Directions for Student Leadership is published by Wiley Periodicals, Inc., 350 Main St., Malden, MA 02148-5020.

Journal Customer Services: For ordering information, claims and any enquiry concerning your journal subscription please go to www.wileycustomerhelp.com/ask or contact your nearest office.
Americas: Email: cs-journals@wiley.com; Tel: +1 781 388 8598 or +1 800 835 6770 (toll free in the USA & Canada).
Europe, Middle East and Africa: Email: cs-journals@wiley.com; Tel: +44 (0) 1865 778315.
Asia Pacific: Email: cs-journals@wiley.com; Tel: +65 6511 8000.
Japan: For Japanese speaking support, Email: cs-japan@wiley.com.
Visit our Online Customer Help available in 7 languages at www.wileycustomerhelp.com/ask

Production Editor: Poornita Jugran (email: pjugran@wiley.com).

Wiley's Corporate Citizenship initiative seeks to address the environmental, social, economic, and ethical challenges faced in our business and which are important to our diverse stakeholder groups. Since launching the initiative, we have focused on sharing our content with those in need, enhancing community philanthropy, reducing our carbon impact, creating global guidelines and best practices for paper use, establishing a vendor code of ethics, and engaging our colleagues and other stakeholders in our efforts. Follow our progress at www.wiley.com/go/citizenship

View this journal online at wileyonlinelibrary.com/journal/he

Wiley is a founding member of the UN-backed HINARI, AGORA, and OARE initiatives. They are now collectively known as Research4Life, making online scientific content available free or at nominal cost to researchers in developing countries. Please visit Wiley's Content Access - Corporate Citizenship site: http://www.wiley.com/WileyCDA/Section/id-390082.html

Printed in the USA by The Sheridan Group.

Address for Editorial Correspondence: Co-editors, Betsy Barefoot and Jillian L. Kinzie, *New Directions for Higher Education*, Email: barefoot@jngi.org

Abstracting and Indexing Services
The Journal is indexed by Academic Search Alumni Edition (EBSCO Publishing); Higher Education Abstracts (Claremont Graduate University); MLA International Bibliography (MLA).

Cover design: Wiley
Cover Images: © Lava 4 images | Shutterstock

For submission instructions, subscription and all other information visit:
wileyonlinelibrary.com/journal/he

Contents

Editors' Notes

The purpose of this monograph is to explore the operation of intellectual property (IP) in higher education, and ways of navigating the changing IP landscape for faculty members and university administrations. For a long time, faculty IP rights to academic work were commonly understood and for the most part unchanging; however, due to technological advancements and the rise of neoliberal policies influenced by academic capitalism (Slaughter & Rhoades, 2004), currently, faculty members find their IP rights being renegotiated, often without their input. Through patents and copyrights, universities and publishers seek to gain a competitive advantage in a market largely dominated by profit generation.

At present, every research university in the United States maintains a formal IP policy. These policies dictate the rights of faculty and students to own and control the academic work they create in the course of attendance or employment. Within these policies, colleges and universities delineate revenue-sharing rights for faculty members to patents, and the rights to own copyright over courseware, including syllabi, lecture notes, and reading lists, as well as their scholarly research articles (Schmidt, 2013). Due to the profit potential of distance education programs and massive open online courses (MOOCs), higher education institutions have begun to claim ownership of course materials traditionally reserved to faculty-creators in the classroom setting. Changes in institutional IP policies may have far-reaching implications for the academic profession, requiring a revisiting of the purposes for, and the values underlying the provision of higher education.

Despite the adoption of profit-driven management practices over the past several decades—a consequence of the academic capitalist ideology—higher education institutions retain certain professional norms and values that set them apart from other profit-generating organizations, such as faculty autonomy and academic freedom, which permit faculty members to control the direction of their research (American Association of University Professors [AAUP], 2013). The AAUP (2013) has argued in a recent draft report that college and university ownership of scholarly works undermines academic freedom and strips faculty members of their autonomy, weakening the academic profession. Recognizing the value of technology in communicating with their audiences, many faculty members are making use of open access outlets for publishing their research. This monograph details the IP barriers that faculty encounter when attempting to share their work.

New Directions for Higher Education, no. 177, Spring 2017 © 2017 Wiley Periodicals, Inc.
Published online in Wiley Online Library (wileyonlinelibrary.com) • DOI: 10.1002/he.20221

This volume is intended for all present and future faculty members, deans, department chairs, administrators, and legal counsel who seek to learn about recent policy trends in IP within higher education institutions, and to prepare themselves for changes within their own institutions. The volume discusses trends in university IP regulation over the past 40 years, examining the utility of IP rights in higher education, and the implications of knowledge ownership in the academic profession.

To understand the evolution of intellectual property issues in academia, it is helpful to first address the rise of a legalistic culture in higher education. In Chapter 1, Lara K. Badke provides an introduction to the legalization of higher education in order to establish context and background for the intellectual property issues explored in subsequent chapters, and to orient the reader to the overarching legal environment in higher education. Beginning with declining state support for higher education in the 1980s and 1990s, universities have had to develop distinctive niches to become self-supporting, and regulators and the courts have become increasingly involved in the management of university affairs. Since then, the judicial deference historically afforded to higher education has eroded, due to growing demand for accountability, consumer protection, due process, student rights, concerns for the public interest, and increasingly commercialized interests. This chapter explores the encroachment of legal rules and regulatory oversight in higher education and their resulting influence over the structure, values, and purpose of higher education. Academia's intellectual property environment has not only been shaped by these significant shifts, but it also contributes to the legalization of modern day higher education: from ownership of federally funded research, to intellectual property regulations that govern commercial exploitation of faculty inventions, and to policies and contractual terms governing property rights.

In Chapter 2, Shafiqa Ahmadi analyzes faculty rights to own, use, and disseminate traditional course materials, like syllabi, readings lists, and lecture notes, as well as the "fair use" doctrine, which dictates the use of third-party materials by faculty in the classroom setting. This chapter also analyzes the unique legal features of educational technologies that distinguish digital courses from traditional classrooms. These topics require a discussion of the difference between public and for-profit institutions, and the legal implications, of university sponsorship of for-profit ventures. The aim of this chapter is to illustrate the legal and practical implications for faculty in the transition from classroom to online teaching, and to make clear that this shift implies more than just a change of venue.

The third chapter, by Molly Kleinman, focuses on the rights of faculty over their scholarly research. Most universities have historically taken a hands-off stance to copyrights in scholarly research. These rights are typically governed by different policies altogether—those of the journal publisher. Traditional academic publishers usually require that authors transfer their copyrights to articles in exchange for publication. This chapter describes the new politics of scholarly publishing, as many faculty members attempt to retain their rights and provide broader access to their work, either by renegotiating terms with established publishers, or circumventing conventional paths to publication in favor of online open access journals. Meanwhile, funders such as the NIH and the Wellcome Trust, along with more than 100 U.S. colleges and universities, have established open access mandates requiring authors to share their work in free online repositories. These controversial approaches offer a number of advantages, such as allowing faculty members to maintain control of their copyrights, promoting greater visibility for research, and improving public access to scholarship. Academic publishing is an important piece of the present discussion because it has implications for scholars' choices of where and how to disseminate their work, and therefore impacts faculty autonomy.

The fourth chapter, by Samantha Bernstein-Sierra, builds from Ahmadi and Kleinman's chapters on technology and open access, and elaborates on the broader movement toward openness in higher education teaching and research, which is tied to the notion of the public good—a key theme in this volume. Openness in the academy refers to the faculty practice of transparency in research activity (Cormier & Siemens, 2010). Values of openness are fundamental to the social mission of the university, and visibility of scholarship is among the most important features to faculty members of conducting academic research. This chapter discusses openness as a social movement in higher education, its origins, and recent developments. From radio "colleges of the air" in the 1920s and 1930s (Matt & Fernandez, 2013), to MIT's open courseware, the driving force behind many educational innovations is the desire to disseminate knowledge freely, and promote equity by reaching populations that would not otherwise have access to higher education. Openness values are crucial to a discussion of IP in higher education because they represent a paradigm that conflicts with the image of the university as a profit-driven enterprise—an image so prevalent in recent years, resulting from academic capitalism. The purpose of this chapter is to shed light on the tension between openness and commodification of research in higher education, and to highlight some areas where this tension is most apparent.

The focus of the fifth chapter, by Gary Rhoades, is collective bargaining agreements in 4-year institutions, and particularly on provisions surrounding distance education and instructional technology. This chapter expands empirically on Ahmadi's chapter, by highlighting recent developments in intellectual property contracting for distance learning materials. The provisions that Rhoades explores address various issues, particularly the question of intellectual property ownership of digital courseware. In examining the 176 contracts nationally (often of state systems of 4-year institutions, as with the California State University System), the chapter analyzes the key factors determining property ownership, and patterns in the extent to which ownership and royalties go to faculty members, as opposed to institutions.

Rhoades also analyzes the contracts in terms of what is missing, in relative terms. For instance, there are several examples of important public policy issues surrounding the push to commercialize high-tech courses, from cost issues (to the student and to the institution) to issues of educational quality and effectiveness for different populations of students. The chapter examines how, in the balance between faculty rights and management claims, some matters of the public interest are largely overlooked, offering another connotation to the question, whose property is it?

The sixth chapter, by Guilbert C. Hentschke, discusses global economic issues dealing primarily with equity and global access to higher education. The importance of intellectual property rights in global economic development has rapidly grown in variety, form, and complexity across countries, regions, and industries and firms. Hentschke's chapter addresses the question: Which among the wide range of IP issues in modern society are central to institutions of higher education? Research and teaching, the two stated missions of most colleges and universities, are characterized by different IP environments, each with independent paths of development. Hentschke characterizes these paths as "commercial grade IP" and "instructional grade IP," and examines the public good aspects of each path as a result of globalization.

The final chapter by Adrianna Kezar synthesizes what changes in IP policy mean for faculty. She suggests that faculty are at a crossroads, with groups such as AAUP suggesting they need to fight for their IP rights, campuses taking siege over those rights, and openness advocates suggesting they reclaim their rights and make all research and teaching materials freely available to serve the public good. Each of these arguments has merit and faculty have to carefully assess which direction they should take. However, if administrative leaders work alone, it is likely that faculty rights will take a backseat to administrative interests. Kezar suggests that collective discussions among faculty (within disciplines, institutions, multicampus systems, or unions) are valuable to assert a position(s) on IP that allows faculty a voice in administrative IP discussions. Although we likely will not have a single faculty stance on IP rights that we have had in the past, it is important that faculty become active participants in conversations about their rights. Kezar's chapter offers ideas for ways that faculty voice can become part of discussions nationally, and suggests some values, resources, and principles that might be part of such conversations. Her chapter also examines ideas of the public good alluded to throughout the volume, raising important questions for faculty leaders.

As the title of this volume suggests, we believe that faculty members should be included in administrative discussions about IP, and involved in institutional IP policy decisions. Further, we believe that the interests of the public good should be raised in discussions about IP, and considered when renegotiating institutional policies. We believe that representing the public interest will allow for more balanced discussions of the benefits and consequences to all stakeholders of higher education.

Samantha Bernstein-Sierra
Adrianna Kezar
Editors

References

American Association of University Professors. (2013). *Defending the freedom to innovate: Faculty intellectual property rights after Stanford v. Roche*. Draft report. Retrieved from http://www.aaup.org/report/defending-freedom-innovate-faculty-intellectual-property-rights-after-stanford-v-roche

Cormier, D., & Siemens, G. (2010). Through the open door: Open courses as research, learning, and engagement. *EDUCAUSE Review, 45*(4), 30–39. Retrieved from http://www.educause.edu/ero/article/through-open-door-open-courses-research-learning-and-engagement

Matt, S., & Fernandez, L. (2013). Before MOOCs, "Colleges of the Air." *The Chronicle of Higher Education.*

Slaughter, S., & Rhoades, G. (2004). *Academic capitalism and the new economy: Markets, states, and higher education.* Baltimore, MD: The Johns Hopkins University Press.

Schmidt, P. (2013). AAUP Sees MOOCs as spawning new threats to professors' intellectual property. *The Chronicle of Higher Education.* Retrieved from http://chronicle.com/article/AAUP-Sees-MOOCs-as-Spawning/139743/

SAMANTHA BERNSTEIN-SIERRA *is an attorney and PhD candidate of urban education policy at the University of Southern California's Rossier School of Education. Her research centers on public/private tensions in higher education, organizational theory, openness in higher education research and teaching, and the future of the academic profession.*

ADRIANNA KEZAR *is professor of higher education at the University of Southern California's Rossier School of Education. Her scholarship focuses on change, leadership, governance, and the changing role of faculty.*

1

A complete discussion of intellectual property (IP), faculty rights, and the public good requires a thorough framing of higher education's legal context, from which the rise of legalistic criteria (or legalization) and current IP regime have grown.

The Legalization of Higher Education

Lara K. Badke

Colleges and universities operate in a complex and ever-changing legal environment, with constraints and opportunities shaped by legal considerations significant factors in organizational functioning and campus relationships (Alger, 2008; Gajda, 2009; McLendon & Hearn, 2006; Olivas, 2005; Toma, 2011). Contemporary intellectual property issues in higher education, centered on the ownership and commodification of knowledge, often conflict with inherent and traditional notions of instructional and scholarly knowledge. The economic, political, and social pressures shaping intellectual property debates combine with legal forces to influence higher education policy and practice. With nearly every activity engaged in by university students, faculty, and staff involving the production or use of original expression (copyright), invention (patent), or brand (trademark), each of which is capable of imparting ownership and profit opportunities, it is impossible for academe to escape intellectual property's reach (Pauken, 2009; Sun & Baez, 2009; Toma, 2011).

Questions of ownership between faculty and their institutions, as well as between academe and industry, are growing more complicated and more contentious. Developing, licensing, and protecting intellectual property rights in higher education often pits individual interests (primarily tied to matters of making, owning, distributing, and capitalizing on knowledge and invention), public interests (consumption of the intellectual good or service), and institutional interests (enabling the commercialization of research, teaching, and other scholarly activities) against each other (Pauken, 2009; Sun & Baez, 2009; Toma, 2011). A prevailing tension, for example, relates to whether inventions should exist to serve society or create economic gain, or even whether these interests are mutually exclusive (American Association for the Advancement of Science, 1934; Mowery & Sampat, 2001;

NEW DIRECTIONS FOR HIGHER EDUCATION, no. 177, Spring 2017 © 2017 Wiley Periodicals, Inc.
Published online in Wiley Online Library (wileyonlinelibrary.com) • DOI: 10.1002/he.20222

Parthasarathy, 2014). As the nature of faculty work and academic research transform higher education, core values, assumptions, and functions of the modern American university are challenged (McGee & Diaz, 2005; Olivas, 2005; Ross, 2012; Slaughter & Leslie, 1997; Slaughter & Rhodes, 2004; Sun & Baez, 2009; Toma, 2011; Welsh, 2000).

The purpose of this chapter is to provide an orientation to the broad legal context shaping the field of modern higher education, linking the legalization of higher education—of which intellectual property is a part—to an environment of diminished academic freedoms and judicial deference to academe. The striking shift of judicial attitudes toward scholarly disputes, including the burgeoning disagreements in assigning ownership and specifying permissible use of ideas, threatens to further restrict the pursuit and transmission of knowledge at the very heart of higher education (Gajda, 2009; McSherry, 2001). By examining significant developments giving rise to the legalization of higher education, the conditions underlying current intellectual property debates and rights can be better understood. Understanding how academic values are diminished as legal scrutiny of university affairs rises is important to the considerations of the intellectual property concerns explored in detail in subsequent chapters.

This chapter surveys social, political, and economic dimensions contributing to the legalization of higher education. I begin by introducing higher education's role as supplier of intellectual property through research, scholarship, and the dissemination of knowledge. Here I consider how higher education's increasingly market-oriented focus has influenced its legal environment. Next, I examine threats of this market orientation to higher education's central values. I argue that as universities begin to operate more like businesses, judicial deference to academic expertise weakens university autonomy. In the next section, I trace the evolution of the legalization of higher education. Highlighting ongoing tensions between outside legal forces and university self-determination, I relate the expanding relationship between the courts and higher education to concerns over intellectual property rights. I then address consequences of the entrepreneurial university on university functioning, particularly through faculty workforce reorganization. In the final section of the chapter, I extend some observations on the importance of intellectual property rights to higher education in a democratic society. I offer these insights to facilitate a greater understanding of the legal environment in which complex intellectual property right debates take place. With the entrepreneurial university bringing academics into more frequent contact with commercial partners and complex laws, and intellectual property as a moneymaker to universities showing no signs of decline, increasing our understanding of the university's legal environment is fundamental to staving off additional threats to academe's defining values.

Legalization and Universities' Growing Business Orientation

Debate abounds surrounding a sense of abandonment of universities' public identity and mission from the rise of a market-oriented university model (Bok, 2003; Gajda, 2009; Lake, 2010; Olivas, 2005; Slaughter, 2001; Slaughter & Leslie, 1997). In addition to raising questions as to the nature and extent of a social compact between universities and society, the commercialization of higher education has been linked with a loss of judicial deference to academic self-governance and academic freedom (Gajda, 2009; Olivas, 2005; Toma, 2011). Though not new, a legalistic environment in higher education—characterized by standardized rule making, the adoption of formal practices, dominance of legalistic decision criteria, heightened concern over litigation, and use of legalistic rhetoric—is on the rise (Edelman & Suchman, 1997; Gajda, 2009; McSherry, 2001; Meyer, 1983; Selznick, 1969; Sitkin & Bies, 1994; Toma, 2011; Weber, 1947). Intellectual property, for example, in which universities seek legal protection over their ideas and brand, is an undeniable strategic asset now occupying a coveted role in the new American university (Bok, 2003; Kirp, 2003; Rhodes, 2001). Given the high stakes involved in legal claims over ownership and other commercial rights relating to intellectual property issues, the impact of legalistic influences on organizational processes and structures, often described as *legalization*, is inevitable (Meyer, 1983; Scott, 1994; Selznick, 1969; Sitkin & Bies, 1994).

Federal policy and a series of court rulings stressing accountability and consumer protection have contributed to this legalized environment, resulting in a tightening of fair use exceptions and shrinking of the public domain. Fair use, essentially the legal use of copyrighted material for a limited and transformative purpose (17 U.S. Code §107—Limitations on exclusive rights: Fair use), has been vaguely defined to enable it to evolve based on changing conditions (Stim, 2010). Works in the public domain are not restricted by copyright, either having never been copyrighted or whose copyright has expired. Such works do not require a license or fee to use. Examples would include the Bible, Mozart's compositions, and mathematical formulae (Stim, 2010). The combination of increasingly restrictive fair use exceptions and a dwindling public domain result in common scholarly materials becoming less accessible and conflicts of interest between public benefit and creator control intensifying (Sun & Baez, 2009; Toma, 2011). To hinder further encroachment on academic values, it is imperative to understand the law's influence on higher education in an increasingly commercialized environment.

Legalization's Encroachment on University Autonomy

Where traditionally courts once steered clear of academic matters, allowing faculty and deans the autonomy to manage internal university affairs,

NEW DIRECTIONS FOR HIGHER EDUCATION • DOI: 10.1002/he

regulatory and legal scrutiny now permeate nearly all aspects of university functioning (Gajda, 2009; Olivas, 2013; Toma, 2011). Between 1997 and 2012 alone, federal regulations of higher education jumped by 56% (American Council on Education, 2015). Legal encroachment into academic matters is considered to be—along with globalization, increased competition, economic pressures, and workforce restructuring—a key contributor to the profound shifts in nature, structure, and values of the modern American university (Ayers, 2005; Gumport, 1993; Paulson & St John, 2002; Saunders, 2010; Slaughter & Rhoades, 2004; Tierney, 1998; Zusman, 2005). Each of these factors has driven university operations and faculty pursuits beyond once central purposes of instruction and scholarship to involvement in market-like behaviors and commercial exploitation of knowledge (Gajda, 2009; Slaughter & Rhoades, 2004).

The infusion of such practices into academic research eroded distinctions that once existed between the academic world and the corporate sector. One consequence of this transformation was that courts became less apt to recognize the professional judgment of educators or defer to institutional autonomy in resolving disputes (Gajda, 2009; Olivas, 2013; Toma, 2011). Offsetting fading state financial support of higher education, universities continued down the path of commercial expansion (Archibald & Feldman, 2006; Cameron, 1983; Gajda, 2009; Paulson & St John, 2002; Saunders, 2010; Slaughter & Rhoades, 2004; Zusman, 2005). The result? Commercial practices on campus grew to an unprecedented size and scope (Bok, 2003; Gajda, 2009; Kirp, 2003; Lake, 2010). The number of patents granted to academic institutions jumped by 1,325% between 1979 and 2000, far exceeding the growth of patents generally (Raj, 2004). While patent licensing in 1991 generated revenue of $123 million for universities, by 2006 that figure had soared to $1.2 billion (Bagley, 2006), with licensing income in 2011 reaching $2.5 billion (autm.net, 2011 Licensing Activity Survey). With an intensifying consumer orientation to higher education as a private good available for purchase further driving commercial expansion, modern day universities have been transformed into immense corporate businesses (Bickel & Lake, 1999; Bok, 2003; Gajda, 2009; Kaplin & Lee, 2006; Lake, 2010; Marske & Vago, 1980; Olivas, 2000, 2005; Saunders, 2010; Slaughter, 2001; Slaughter & Leslie, 1997; Toma, 2011). One of the inevitable results of this shift: a watershed juncture between campus and courts leading to an increase in the legalization of higher education.

The term *legalization* has been treated with different and sometimes conflicting connotations (Friedman, 1975; Meyer, 1981, 1983; Roth, Sitkin, & House, 1994; Scott, 1994; Selznick, 1969; Sitkin & Bies, 1993, 1994; Weber, 1947; Yudof, 1981). Drawing on the work of organizational scholars who examined the close association of law and organizations, legalization can be understood to refer to the acts of outside forces (traditionally presented in the guise of legislation, regulation, and litigation) that affect the organization (such as ownership over courseware and scholarly research

NEW DIRECTIONS FOR HIGHER EDUCATION • DOI: 10.1002/he

articles), and those in it (faculty, students, and administrators), in relation to its legal culture and environment (balancing of rights as knowledge assets are produced, protected, and made profitable) (Selznick, 1969; Sitkin & Bies, 1994). Such outside acts often transcend routine compliance with legal requirements (e.g., exceeding responsibilities under the Copyright Act) and create opposition between education and society (questioning whether academic inventions should serve a public good or proprietary financial gain) (Jasanoff, 1985; Meyer, 1981, 1983). Further complicating the legal environment in higher education are new and unsettling forms of informal lawmaking. Policy making initiated through ballot initiatives, insurance policy restrictions, and commercial law practices transform an already volatile legal landscape, with universities having to understand and adapt to additional legal obligations (Olivas, 2000, 2005, 2013; Toma, 2011).

Evolution of the Legalization of Higher Education

Literature addressing the phenomenon of legalization in higher education reveals a strong historical inclination by the courts to steer clear of campus disputes (ownership of course materials, for example), allowing universities to manage their own affairs (Gajda, 2009; Kaplin, 1985; Munn, 1998). Routine academic disputes were settled internally among a community of scholars with high degrees of personal interaction, organizational purpose, and shared professional norms and values (Berdhahl, 1991; Burnett & Matthews, 1982; Gajda, 2009; Goodman, 1962; Hardy, 1992; Kaplin, 1985; Millett, 1962; Munn, 1998; Warters, 1998). Higher education was considered a unique enterprise "far too delicate and complex for involvement by outsiders" (Munn, 1998, p. 36) who would "be ignorant of the special agreements and sensitivities underpinning [the academic] environment" (Kaplin, 1985, p. 4). Federal and state governments were reluctant to establish laws, regulations, or obligations that directly impacted the daily operations of a university (Gajda, 2009; Munn, 1998). Institutional management was effectively maintained through normative practice and consensual agreement. Today, fueled by a weakened social compact between universities and society, diminished respect for university decision-making autonomy, and an individual rights mindset, a remarkable number of disagreements in academe end up in court, displacing academic judgment in internal affairs with that of a judge or jury (Gajda, 2009; Helms, 1987; Munn, 1998; Schauer, 2006; Yudof, 1981).

A shift in legislative and judicial attitudes toward higher education rapidly expanded with growing civil rights awareness (Bickel & Lake, 1999; Munn, 1998; Yudof, 1981). An increase in student rights, campus protests, and organizing movements created a shift in collegial and deferential attitudes, and an inundation of lawsuits demanding judicial review of university decisions. Courts became forums for novel causes of litigation not heard of a decade earlier, such as complaints over grades, tenure denial, even office allocation (Burnett & Matthews, 1982; Gajda, 2009). Broader and less welcome forms of judicial oversight of university decisions had begun. These were most apparent in the growing duty placed upon the university in the form of contract law (a student arguing she or he did not receive the quality of education paid for, for example) and tort law (a professor's conduct or an unreasonable university policy causing a student harm). University management was subjected to greater scrutiny from its constituents, who turned to the courts to voice their objections to academic differences. Where academic abstention doctrines once protected university decision-making autonomy, judges were now increasingly receptive to mediating campus conflicts (Gajda, 2009; Lake, 2005).

Following an era of unprecedented civil rights, affirmative action, political discontent, and judicial battles over campus management pitting universities against students, the 1980s ushered in additional legalization by stepping up legislative reforms and expanding individuals' standing to sue universities. Of particular relevance to the evolution of intellectual property rights in higher education was the introduction in 1980 of the Bayh–Dole Act and amendments to the Copyright Act (Sun & Baez, 2009). Not only was the growth and profitability of computer software exploding as the Patent and Trademark Office began issuing patents to software, but universities could now also patent and license the results of federally funded research. Prior to the Bayh–Dole legislation, the rights to inventions created with federal funding remained with the government, who licensed fewer than 5% of patentable inventions (Schacht, 2000). Proponents of the Bayh–Dole Act argued that the results of university-based discoveries could promote the public good by improving lives, encouraging innovation, promoting the progress of science, increasing competition, and stimulating the economy. The legislation ultimately created new pathways and financial incentives for universities to commercialize their research (S. Rep. No. 96–480, 1979; 35 USC §200). This regulation for the "public good" was not without ulterior motives. Congress was concerned at the time with a stagnant economy and declining industrial competitiveness (Stevens, 2004). Universities found themselves a convenient target in the economic and political arguments for change.

Continuing legislative reforms coupled with precedent setting cases of aggrieved parties resorting to courts to resolve intellectual property disputes resulted in a growing "propertization" of academic work (Gajda, 2009; McSherry, 2001). The 1989 New York federal appeals case of *Weissmann v. Freeman*, for example, illustrated a marked shift of judicial attitudes in academic disputes. The trial court dismissed the dispute, over scholarly credit between a junior associate and her prominent mentor, based on academic norms. The court determined the root cause of the dispute to be misguided ego, and argued such academic quarrels did not belong in the courts. The appellate court, however, overruled the lower court's deference to academic norms and strictly applied the Copyright Act to the authorship dispute. It also recognized academic identity as property. Extending the exchange and ownership of knowledge beyond patents and copyright, Weissmann introduced a new academic property claim of name and identity misappropriation (unauthorized use of a scholar's valuable identity). Essentially, the court broadened the causes of action in which customary norms of academic collaboration could be challenged (Gajda, 2009; McSherry, 2001; Weissmann, 1989). This propertization of academic work, aptly illustrated in modern lawsuits questioning ownership of lecture materials (by professor, institution, or student), for example, situates scholarship and pedagogy at the center of a market economy that allows courts the leeway to assign ownership and specify permissible uses of ideas and knowledge at the heart of the academic enterprise (Blumenstyk, 1999; Gajda, 2009; McSherry, 2001). The changing circumstances influencing ownership rights to academic work did not occur in a vacuum. Concurrently, other pressures were contributing to higher education's market transformation in which intellectual property, once regarded in academe as a necessary evil, evolved as a virtue and institutional moneymaker (Bok, 2003; Gajda, 2009; Kirp, 2003).

Effects of the Entrepreneurial University

As increasing importance was placed on universities to bring innovations to market, a shift in university culture began. The massification of higher education brought increased enrollments, expanded the number and type of learning institutions, and saw increases in federal research funding. Whereas a societal benefit of higher education was to educate the masses on the one hand, public financial support was being withdrawn on the other. Between 1980 and 1993, state funding for public institutions fell by 8.8%. Government funding as a percentage of all revenue sources for higher education declined by almost 10% (Gumport, Iannozzi, Shaman, & Zemsky, 1997). The steady decline in government support necessitated that universities develop distinctive niches and become self-supporting. Revenue generation and entrepreneurial ambition fueled the expansion of inventions, virtual education, and corporate partnerships. As university research became more commodified, commercial practices on campus swelled, enabling universities to pursue their academic missions through external financing and expansion. This move toward academic capitalism had the unforeseen effects of fueling workforce reform and contributing to the growing legalization of higher education (Gajda, 2009; Olivas, 2005; Rhoades, 1996; Slaughter, 2001; Somers & Somers-Willett, 2002).

Heightened research pressures and teaching loads were transforming faculty structures. Not only were entrepreneurial expectations of faculty rising, but the organizational complexity to manage research programs and functions was rapidly expanding (Gumport et al., 1997). Changes to faculty composition became a contributing factor in the shift in organizational control away from faculty toward administrators. Shared governance and collegial decision making, systems characteristic of higher education prior to the growth of late modernity, had given way to more hierarchical and political decision-making models (Kezar & Eckel, 2004; Saunders, 2010). As the nature of faculty work and faculty composition changed from tenure-track faculty engaged simultaneously in teaching, research, and service to nontenure track teaching or research or service-only roles, the market-driven transformation of academic work created a stratification in academic employment and job security (Rhoades, 2004; Saunders, 2010; Toma, 2011).

Across the field as a whole, tenured professors began to slowly disappear from the higher education landscape, with nontenure track adjuncts outnumbering their tenured colleagues' ranks (Donoghue, 2008). The tightening academic job market, in conjunction with power imbalances, poor working conditions, and few contractual rights created an environment in which contingent faculty had little other recourse than to resort to litigation when aggrieved (Burnett & Matthews, 1982; Gajda, 2009). Ownership disputes led institutions to argue that work produced within the scope of faculty's paid university employment (known as the work-made-for-hire doctrine) resided with them, the employer, not the faculty member (Toma, 2011). As the number of contingent faculty denied the protection of academic freedom grew, so did the amount of litigation on related issues (Euben, 2004). Administrators were inconsistently applying institutional policies based on faculty rank. Disparity between tenured and contingent faculty created a risk management imperative for the institution. Universities could no longer demonstrate adherence to their own rules created to safeguard unique academic circumstances. How then could they expect to insulate themselves from the courts on the basis of substantive and procedural fairness? Faculty increasingly turned to the courts to resolve discrimination, First Amendment (academic freedom, free speech), and property claims to assert their rights. These claims opened up new directions for external judicial supervision and control of the intellectual life of a university, further displacing traditional and socially beneficial academic norms of sharing and collaboration (Gajda, 2009; Kezar, Maxey, & Badke, 2014; Toma, 2011).

Importance of Intellectual Property Rights to Higher Education in a Democratic Society

The amalgamation of such factors as the commercialization of higher education and transformation of the academic workforce pose threats to academic freedom because of the breakdown in the basic social compact underlying higher education. The effectiveness of the university is premised on a covenant struck between the university and the general public under which society financially supports the university and grants it great autonomy. In return, the university invests its resources and freedoms to serve the larger public interest (Finkin & Post, 2009; Rhodes, 2001). The public, through government policy, has seemingly broken its end of the bargain by withdrawing financial support and increasing regulatory oversight. Universities have adapted by raising tuition and brokering new commodities—everything from patents to executive education partnerships—resulting in a sense of abandonment of their public identity and mission. Institutional policies developed in support of this entrepreneurial direction often create a chilling effect on academic freedom under the guise of "innovation" (Toma, 2011). Abandoning the public purpose that once personified research universities, academic freedom rights to pursue controversial work diminish in favor of entrepreneurial ambition. Such threats to academic freedom are particularly acute with an increasing number of contingent faculty operating with neither constitutional nor contractual protections. Tenured faculty are also not immune to shifts in academic freedom protections, with course content and delivery undermined as work-for-hire within the scope of employment shifts ownership rights to the university. Balancing the legitimate interests of all stakeholders—the public's use and enjoyment of content, the university's efforts to advance innovation and seek new funding streams, faculty's right to their own work and creations—are further complicated as traditional rights of self-governance face the rising tide of courts asserting themselves into the once unique environment of academic judgments (Gajda, 2009; Toma, 2011).

In today's increasingly regulated and commercialized academic environment, universities' potential liability for infringement of intellectual property rights looms large. The line between fair use of copyrighted material and copyright infringement, for example, is precarious. Universities must simultaneously balance moral and pecuniary rights of scholarship and intellectual property with monitoring and enforcement obligations, such as removal of materials once the institution is informed of copyright infringement (Toma, 2011). Universities possess the power to influence legal compliance and shape norms as they select, interpret, and challenge laws (Edelman, Fuller, & Mara-Drita, 2001; Edelman, Leachman, & McAdam, 2010; Edelman & Suchman, 1997; Scott, 1994; Suchman & Edelman, 1996). If universities fail to influence the progression of intellectual property laws and practices that affect higher education and its interests, rival groups' (pharmaceutical companies influencing programs for the continuing education of medical practitioners, for example; or technology companies specializing in Internet-related services owning and controlling knowledge) ability to shape the law for purposes other than to advance teaching, learning, and research strengthens. The evolution of the legalization of higher education paints a picture of a higher education landscape marked by increasingly divisive interests, polarizing events, legal pressures, and threats to academic values. With changes in the legal environment creating incentives for competitive advantage (Bagley 2008, 2010; Bird, 2008, 2011), it is incumbent upon higher education to advocate on behalf of the importance of intellectual property rights to the critical roles of teaching, learning, and research in a democratic society. Without taking such a proactive stand, the free and open exchange of ideas underlying higher education's central values risk further erosion as the intrusion of outside forces that affect the organization, and those in it, in relation to its legal culture and environment, continues to grow.

References

American Association for the Advancement of Science. (1934). *The protection by patents of scientific discoveries.* New York, NY: Author.

American Council on Education. (2015). *Recalibrating regulation of colleges and universities: Report of the Task Force on Federal Regulation of Higher Education.* Washington, DC: Author. http://www.acenet.edu/news-room/Documents/Higher-Education-Regulations-Task-Force-Report.pdf

Alger, J. A. (2008). Legal issues for academic leaders. *Effective Practices for Academic Leaders, 3*(2), 1–14.

Archibald, R. B., & Feldman, D. H. (2006). State higher education spending and the tax revolt. *The Journal of Higher Education, 77*(4), 618–644.

Ayers, D. F. (2005). Neoliberal ideology in community college mission statements: A critical discourse analysis. *The Review of Higher Education, 28*(4), 527–549.

Bagley, M. A. (2006). Academic discourse and proprietary rights: Putting patents in their proper place. *Boston College Law Review, 47*(2), 217–274.

Bagley, C. E. (2008). Winning legally: The value of legal astuteness. *The Academy of Management Review, 33*(2), 378–390.

Bagley, C. E. (2010). What's law got to do with it? Integrating law and strategy. *American Business Law Journal, 47*(4), 587–639.

Berdhahl, R. O. (1991). Shared academic governance and external constraints. In M. W. Peterson, E. E. Chaffed, & T. H. White (Eds.), *Organization and academic governance in higher education* (4th ed.). Needham Heights, MA: Ginned Press.

Bickel, R. D., & Lake, P. F. (1999). *The rights and responsibilities of the modern university: Who assumes the risks of college life?* Durham, NC: Carolina Academic Press.

Bird, R. C. (2008). Pathways of legal strategy. *Stanford Journal of Law, Business & Finance, 14*(1), 1–41.

Bird, R. C. (2011). Law, strategy and competitive advantage. *American Business Law Journal, 47.*

Blumenstyk, G. (1999, October 1). Putting class notes on the web: Are companies stealing lectures? *The Chronicle of Higher Education,* A31.

Bok, D. (2003). *Universities in the marketplace: The commercialization of higher education.* Princeton, NJ: Princeton University Press.

Burnett, C. W., & Matthews, W. L. (1982). The legalistic culture in American higher education. *College and University, 57*(2), 197–207.

Cameron, K. (1983). Strategic responses to conditions of decline: Higher education and the private sector. *The Journal of Higher Education, 54*(4), 359–380.

Donoghue, F. (2008). *The last professors: The corporate university and the fate of the humanities.* New York, NY: Fordham University Press.

Edelman, L. B., Fuller, S. R., & Mara-Drita, I. (2001). Diversity rhetoric and the managerialization of law. *American Journal of Sociology, 106*(6), 1589–1641.

Edelman, L. B., Leachman, G., & McAdam, D. (2010). On law, organizations, and social movements. *The Annual Review of Law and Social Science, 6,* 653–658.

Edelman, L. B., & Suchman, M. C. (1997). The legal environment of organizations. *Annual Review of Sociology, 23,* 479–515.

Euben, D. R. (2004). Legal watch: Contingent faculty and the courts. *Academe*. http://www.aaup.org/AAUP/pubsres/academe/2004/JF/Col/lw.htm

Finkin, M. W., & Post, R. C. (2009). *For the common good: Principles of American academic freedom*. New Haven, CT: Yale University Press.

Friedman, L. M. (1975). *The legal system: A social science perspective*. New York, NY: Russell Sage Foundation.

Gajda, A. (2009). *The trials of academe: The new era of campus litigation*. Cambridge, MA: Harvard University Press.

Goodman, P. (1962). *The community of scholars*. New York, NY: Random House.

Gumport, P. (1993). The contested terrain of academic program reduction. *The Journal of Higher Education, 64*, 283–311.

Gumport, P. J., Iannozzi, M., Shaman, S., & Zemsky, R. (1997). *Trends in United States higher education: From massification to post massification*. National Center for Postsecondary Improvement. Stanford University. http://web.stanford.edu/group/ncpi/documents/pdfs/1-04_massification.pdf

Hardy, C. (1992). Retrenchment strategies in two Canadian universities: A political analysis. *Canadian Journal of Administrative Sciences, 9*(3), 180–191.

Helms, L. B. (1987). Patterns of litigation in postsecondary education: A case law study. *Journal of College and University Law, 14*(1), 99–119.

Jasanoff, S. (1985). The misrule of law at OSHA. In D. Nelkin (Ed.), *The language of risk: Conflicting perspectives on occupational health* (pp. 155–177). Beverly Hills, CA: Sage.

Kaplin, W. A. (1985). *The law of higher education: A comprehensive guide to legal implications of administrative decision making* (2nd ed.). San Francisco, CA: Jossey-Bass.

Kaplin, W. A., & Lee, B. A. (2006). *The law of higher education* (4th ed.). San Francisco, CA: Jossey-Bass.

Kezar, A. J., & Eckel, P. D. (2004). Meeting today's governance challenges: A synthesis of the literature and examination of a future agenda for scholarship. *The Journal of Higher Education, 75*(4), 371–399.

Kezar, A., Maxey, D., & Badke, L. (2014). *The imperative for change: Fostering understanding of the necessity of changing non-tenure-track faculty policies and practices*. The Delphi Project on the Changing Faculty and Student. http://www.uscrossier.org/pullias/wp-content/uploads/2013/02/IMPERATIVE-FOR-CHANGE_WEB.pdf

Kirp, D. L. (2003). *Shakespeare, Einstein, and the bottom line: The marketing of higher education*. Cambridge, MA: Harvard University Press.

Lake, P. F. (2005). Private law continues to come to campus: Rights and responsibilities revisited. *Journal of College and University Law, 31*, 621.

Lake, P. F. (2010, December 5). What's next for private universities? Accountability. *The Chronicle of Higher Education*. http://chronicle.com/article/Whats-Next-for-Private/125599/

Marske, C. E., & Vago, S. (1980). Law and dispute processing in the academic community. *Judicature, 64*(4), 165–175.

McGee, P., & Diaz, V. (2005). Planning for the digital classroom and distributed learning: Policies and planning for online instructional resources. *Planning for Higher Education, 33*(4), 12–24.

McLendon, M. K., & Hearn, J. C. (2006). Mandated openness in public higher education: A field study of state sunshine laws and institutional governance. *The Journal of Higher Education, 77*(4), 645–683.

McSherry, C. (2001). *Who owns academic work? Battling for control of intellectual property*. Cambridge, MA: Harvard University Press.

Meyer, J. W. (1981). *Organizational factors affecting legalization in education* (Report No. IFG-PR-81-B10). Stanford, CA: Institute for Research on Educational Finance and Governance.

Meyer, J. W. (1983). Organizational factors affecting legalization in education. In J. W. Meyer & W. R. Scott (Eds.), *Organizational environments: Ritual and rationality* (pp. 217–232). San Francisco, CA: Jossey-Bass.

Millett, J. D. (1962). *The academic community.* New York, NY: McGraw-Hill.

Mowery, D. C., & Sampat, B. N. (2001). Patenting and licensing university inventions: Lessons from the history of the Research Corporation. *Industrial and Corporate Change, 10*(2), 317–355.

Munn, R. L. (1998). The attorney-administrator relationship: A perspective on institutional decision making and power. *NASPA Journal, 36*(1), 35–47.

Olivas, M. A. (2000). Introduction: Intellectual property on campus, computers, copyright, and cyberspace. *Journal of College and University Law, 27*(1).

Olivas, M. A. (2005). The legal environment: The implementation of legal change on campus. In P. G. Altbach, R. O. Berdahl, & P. Gumport (Eds.), *American higher education in the twenty-first century* (pp. 226–252). Baltimore, MD: John Hopkins University Press.

Olivas, M. A. (2013). *Suing alma mater.* Baltimore, MD: Johns Hopkins University Press.

Parthasarathy, S. (2014). *Inventing democracy through the life form patent battles in the United States and Europe.* Chicago, IL: University of Chicago Press.

Pauken, P. D. (2009). Intellectual property. In C. J. Russo (Ed.), *Encyclopedia of law and higher education.* Thousand Oaks, CA: Sage, http://dx.doi.org.proxy.lib.umich.edu/10.4135/ 9781412969024

Paulson, M. B., & St John, E. P. (2002). Social class and college costs: Examining the financial nexus between college choice and persistence. *The Journal of Higher Education, 73*(2), 189–236.

Raj, A. K. (2004). The increasingly proprietary nature of publicly funded biomedical research. In D. G. Stein (Ed.), *Buying in or selling out? The commercialization of the American research university* (pp. 117–126). New Brunswick, NJ: Rutgers University Press.

Rhoades, G. (1996). Reorganizing the faculty workforce for flexibility: Part-time professional labor. *The Journal of Higher Education, 67*(6), 636–670.

Rhodes, F. T. (2001). *The creation of the future: The role of the American university.* Ithaca, NY: Cornell University Press.

Ross, S. (2012). Intellectual property policies in academe: Issues and concerns with digital scholarship. In B. R. Bernhardt, L. H. Hinds, & K. T. Strauch (Eds.), *Accentuate the positive: Charleston conference proceedings* (pp. 397–400). West Lafayette, IN: Purdue University Press.

Roth, N. L., Sitkin, S. B., & House, A. (1994). Stigma as a determinant of legalization. In S. B. Sitkin & R. J. Bies (Eds.), *The legalistic organization* (pp. 137–168). Thousand Oaks, CA: Sage.

Saunders, D. B. (2010). Neoliberal ideology and public higher education in the United States. *Journal for Critical Education Policy Studies, 8*(1), 42–77.

Schacht, W. H. (2000). *Patent ownership and federal research and development (R&D): A discussion on the Bayh–Dole Act and the Stevenson-Wydler Act.* Washington, DC: Congressional Research Service.

Schauer, F. (2006). Is there a right to academic freedom? *Colorado Law Review, 77*(4), 907.

Scott, W. R. (1994). Law and organizations. In S. B. Sitkin & R. J. Bies (Eds.), *The legalistic organization* (pp. 3–18). Thousand Oaks, CA: Sage.

Selznick, P. (1969). *Law, society, and industrial justice.* New York, NY: Russell Sage Foundation.

Sitkin, S. B., & Bies, R. J. (1993). The legalistic organization: Definitions, dimensions, and dilemmas. *Organization Science, 4*(3), 345–351.

Sitkin, S. B., & Bies, R. J. (1994). The legalization of organizations: A multi-theoretical perspective. In S. B. Sitkin & R. J. Bies (Eds.), *The legalistic organization* (pp. 19–49). Thousand Oaks, CA: Sage.

Slaughter, S. (2001). Professional values and the allure of the market. *Academe, 87*(5), 22–26.

Slaughter, S., & Leslie, L. L. (1997). *Academic capitalism: Politics, policies, and the entrepreneurial university.* Baltimore, MD: The John Hopkins University Press.

Slaughter, S., & Rhoades, G. (2004). *Academic capitalism and the new economy: Markets, state, and higher education.* Baltimore, MD: The Johns Hopkins University Press.

Somers, P., & Somers-Willett, S. B. (2002). Collateral damage: Faculty free speech in America after 9/11. *Teachers College Record.* http://www.tcrecod.org/library ID Number: 11004

Stevens, A. J. (2004). The enactment of Bayh–Dole. *The Journal of Technology Transfer, 29*(1), 93–99. doi:10.1023/B:JOTT.0000011183.40867.52

Stim, R. (2010). *Getting permission: How to license & clear copyrighted materials online & off.* Berkeley, CA: NOLO.

Suchman, M. C., & Edelman, L. B. (1996). Legal rational myths: The new institutionalism and the law and society tradition. *Law & Social Inquiry, 21*(4), 903–941.

Sun, J. C., & Baez, B. (2009). Intellectual property in the information age: Knowledge as commodity and its legal implications for higher education. *ASHE Higher Education Reporter*, (34), 4.

Tierney, W. G. (1998). Tenure is dead, long live tenure. In W. G. Tierney (Ed.), *The responsive university: Restructuring for high performance* (pp. 38–61). Baltimore, MD: The Johns Hopkins University Press.

Toma, J. D. (2011). *Managing the entrepreneurial university: Legal issues and commercial realities.* New York, NY: Routledge.

Warters, W. W. (1998). *The history of campus mediation systems: Research and practice.* http://law.gsu.edu/cncr/pdf/papers/99-1Waterspap.pdf

Weber, M. (1947). *The theory of social and economic organization.* New York, NY: Free Press.

Weissmann, v. Freeman, 684 F. Supp. 1248 (S.D.N.Y. 1988), *rev'd* 868 F.2d 1313 (2d Cir), *cert. denied*, 493 U.S. 883 (1989).

Welsh, J. F. (2000). Course ownership in a new technological context: The dynamics of problem definition. *The Journal of Higher Education, 71*(6), 668–699.

Yudof, M. G. (1981). Legalization of dispute resolution, distrust of authority, and organizational theory: Implementing due process for students in the public schools. *Wisconsin Law Review, 1981*(5), 891–923.

Zusman, A. (2005). Challenges facing higher education in the twenty-first century. *American higher education in the twenty-first century: Social, political, and economic challenges, 2,* 115–160.

LARA K. BADKE holds a doctor of philosophy in higher education (2016) from the University of Michigan. Her work addresses complexities in higher education organization and management in relation to legal pressures. Lara also earned a juris doctor (1997) from the University of Windsor.

2

Ownership of traditional courseware is vested in the faculty. In the digital forum, however, under the Copyright Act of 1976, case law, and institutional policy ownership maybe vested in the institution.

Faculty Rights to Courses and Digital Courseware

Shafiqa Ahmadi

With the use of technology, traditional brick and mortar classrooms in college settings are transformed into virtual classrooms that provide access to students anywhere in the world. Although this is great for students, it does present uncertainty for faculty who create and teach online courses. Faculty's ownership rights to these courses are diminished, and at times are nonexistent. Traditional copyright and ownership law does not fit neatly into today's vastly expanding distance education. Written institutional policies vesting copyright and ownership in the institution has replaced the custom and tradition of copyright ownership of faculty.

Primarily through a legal analysis, this chapter attempts to identify and understand faculty rights to own, use, and disseminate traditional course materials, like syllabi, reading lists, and lecture notes, in traditional classroom settings as well as in distance education. The first part of this chapter discusses intellectual property, which includes: copyright, ownership, work-for-hire, employee and scope of employment, teacher exception, and institutional policy and then focuses on traditional and distance education. The next section provides an overview of various types of massive open online courses (MOOCs), and concludes with a discussion of legal and practical implications for faculty as they transition from face-to-face to online teaching.

Intellectual Property: Copyright

On September 17, 1787, the U.S. Constitution was signed. The Constitution grants Congress the power "To Promote the Progress of Sciences and useful Arts, by securing for limited Times to Authors and Inventors the exclusive Right to their respective Writings and Discoveries" (U.S. Const. art. I, §1787). Shortly thereafter, Congress passed the Copyright Act of

NEW DIRECTIONS FOR HIGHER EDUCATION, no. 177, Spring 2017   © 2017 Wiley Periodicals, Inc.
Published online in Wiley Online Library (wileyonlinelibrary.com) • DOI: 10.1002/he.20223

25

1790, which provided more security for authors and inventors. In 1976, the Copyright Act of 1790 was revised; it details copyright protection for "original works of authorship fixed in any tangible medium of expression" (1976, §102(a)). "Originality" was defined by the Supreme Court as "the work [that] was independently created by the author ... and that it possesses at least some degree of creativity" (*Feist Publ'ns, Inc. v. Rural Telephone Services Company*, 1991, p. 345). The term fixed in the Copyright Act of 1976 is defined as "work that must be sufficiently embodied in a copy or a phonorecord—by or under the author's authority—to allow its perception, reproduction, or communication" (Daniel & Pauken, 2015, p. 476). When discussing copyright, ownership and work-for-hire are two areas that must be addressed in order to better understand faculty rights.

Ownership.   The general rule regarding ownership is established under section 201 of the Copyright Act (1976). It states that unless the parties have agreed otherwise, "copyright protection vests initially in the author or authors of the work" (Daniel & Pauken, 2015, p. 488). In most cases, the author is the "individual (or individuals) who actually created and fixed the work" (Priest, 2012, p. 401). Additionally, the Copyright Act of 1976 states that an author is the "one who makes an original contribution that is 'greater than trivial'" (1976, §201).

Given the definition of original works of authorship that is fixed, generally, faculty in postsecondary institutions have the right to own, use, and disseminate traditional course materials such as syllabi, reading lists, and lecture notes that they have created. Regarding faculty ownership over course materials, legal precedent was set as far back as 1825 in London in the case of *Abernethy v. Hutchinson* (1825). In this case, a surgeon delivered lectures, while a student took notes and published it. The surgeon sued for infringement and the court held that a lecturer owns his verbal expression whether it is formally published. In the United States (U.S.), courts have decided in a similar vein. For instance, in the case *Williams v. Weisser* (1969), a private publisher hired a student to take notes during lectures at the University of California Los Angeles (UCLA). Because the faculty member had not given permission to the student, he sued for injunctive relief and damages. The defense argued that even though the faculty member had not given permission, UCLA had given tacit permission. In rejecting this argument, the court stated that UCLA could not give permission to something that it did not own, and thus authorship was vested in the faculty member.

Generally speaking, authorship is vested in the individual who created and fixed the original work in a way that is "greater than trivial." There is an exception to this general rule, and that is, the doctrine of work-for-hire (Priest, 2012; U.S. Copyright Act, 1976).

Work-for-Hire.   The concept and definition of authorship varies, especially when "work-for-hire" is taken into account. Section 201(b) of the Copyright Act defines work-for-hire as "work prepared by an employee within the scope of his or her employment" (U.S. Copyright Act, 1976,

§201(b)). Decades before work-for-hire was enshrined in the Copyright Act of 1976, it was first introduced in the case of *Colliery Engineers Co. v. United Correspondence Schools Co.* (C.C.D. N.Y. 1899), where the employee was "a salaried emplye [sic] of complainant, *inter alia*, to compile, prepare, and revise the instruction and question paper" (p. 152). In this case, the court found that "the literary product of such work became the property of the complainant," the employer (*Colliery Engineer Co. v. United Correspondence Schools Co.*, C.C.D. N.Y. 1899, p. 152). Four years later, the Supreme Court in *Bleistein v. Donaldson Lithographing Co.* (1903) found that the employer can sue for infringement because "designs belonged to [the employer] having been produced by a person employed and paid by the [employer] in their establishment to make those very things" (p. 239). Soon after the Bleistein decision, Congress codified the work-for-hire doctrine in the Copyright Act of 1909 (Laughlin, 2000). The Copyright Act of 1909 defined author to include "an employer in the case of a work for hire" (Copyright Act of 1909, 1909, p. 349).

When Congress revised the copyright law and passed the Copyright Act of 1976, it expanded the definition of work-for-hire doctrine to include "a work prepared by an employee within the scope of his or her employment" (1976, §101). Section 201 includes, *inter alia*:

> In the case of work for hire, the employer or other persons for whom the work was prepared is considered the author for purposes of this title, and unless the parties have expressly agreed otherwise in a written instrument signed by them, owns all of the rights comprised in the copyright. (Copyright Act of 1976).

While the Copyright Act of 1976 provides much detail about work-for-hire, it does not define "employee" or "scope of employment." In fact, "employee" and "scope of employment" is mostly defined through in case law.

Employee and Scope of Employment. In *Community for Creative Non-Violence (CCNV) v. Reid (Reid)* (1989), CCNV, a homeless charity, paid James Earl Reid for a statue that he sculpted, which depicted the plight of homeless people for a Christmas pageant in Washington, DC. CCNV members visited Reid's studio as he made the statue, gave suggestions and directions about its appearance. CCNV paid Reid the final installment on delivery. The parties had not discussed copyright ownership. Shortly after delivery both parties filed competing copyright claims. In this case, the Supreme Court held that when evaluating whether to classify an individual as an employee or not, the Restatement Second of Agency Law should be consulted (Priest, 2012). The Supreme Court noted, "in the past, when Congress has used the term 'employee' without defining it, we have concluded that Congress intended to describe the conventional master-servant relationship as understood by common-law agency doctrine" (*Community* *for Creative Non-Violence v. Reid*, 1989, p. 743–748). The Court offered a multifactor balancing test to consider when determining employee status and scope of employment to include: (1) whether the employer has a right to control the manner and means by which the work is completed; (2) the skill required to complete the work; (3) the source of the materials and tools used to perform the work; (4) where the work was performed; (5) length of relationship between the parties; (6) whether the hiring party could assign additional projects to the hired party; (7) extent of hired party's discretion over when and how long to work; (8) method of payment; (9) the hired party's role in hiring and paying assistants; (10) whether the work was part of the hiring party's regular business; (11) whether the hiring party is in business; (12) whether the hiring party paid employee benefits; and (13) tax treatment of the hired party (whether or not the employer withheld taxes) (*Community for Creative Non-Violence v. Reid*, 1989). The Supreme Court held that Reid was an independent contractor, not an employee, thus the sculpture was not work-for-hire and the copyright was vested in Reid.

Although Reid's balancing test has 12 factors, other courts have found that not all of the factors should be weighed equally, nor are all the factors applicable in each case. Instead, only some factors may be significant in all situations. For instance, in *Aymes v. Bonelli* (1992), Bonelli hired Aymes to create computer programs. There was no written agreement over who owned the copyright on the programs. Aymes did most of his work in an office at Bonelli's company, but sometimes was paid by the project, and sometimes by the hour. Bonelli did not pay Aymes' health insurance, or withhold taxes. After a dispute, both Bonelli and Aymes claimed copyright on the computer programs. Bonelli argued that Aymes was an employee of the company, and so the computer programs were work-for-hire, so Bonelli owned it. Using Section 101(2), which states that work produced by independent contractors is only a work-for-hire if the parties expressly agree to it in writing, Aymes argued that he was an independent contractor, and therefore the program was not a work-for-hire. The Court of Appeals for the Second Circuit found that the programs created by the programmer, Aymes, was not a work-for-hire under the Copyright Act of 1976, vesting the programmer with ownership of the copyright as author of the program. The Appellate Court reasoned that only 5 out of the 12 factors of Reid were relevant: (1) the hiring party's right to control the manner and means of creation; (2) the skill required; (3) the provision of employee benefits; (4) the tax treatment of the hired party; and (5) whether the hiring party has the right to assign additional projects to the hired party (*Aymes v. Bonelli*, 1992).

At first glance, under Reid's balancing factors, it appears that faculty in postsecondary institutions are employees (Priest, 2012). That is, postsecondary institutions provide faculty tools and materials, such as books, office, computer, access to library, research assistants, administrative assistant, and so on. Postsecondary institutions also give faculty salary, health insurance, and withhold federal and state taxes. But, not all of Reid's factors point to an employee–employer relationship. For instance, when considering the factor—"control the manner and means by which the work is completed"—postsecondary institutions rarely, if at all, tell faculty how to teach a course, which pedagogical tools to use, or what topics faculty should research (Priest, 2012).

Even if an employer–employee relationship is deemed to exist, the work is considered work-for-hire "only if the work was created within the scope of employment" (Priest, 2012, p. 402). To determine whether the work was created within the scope of employment, courts have consulted Section 228 of the Restatement Second of Agency (1958) that includes: (1) whether the work was of a "kind the employee is hired to perform"; (2) it "occurs substantially within the authorized time and space limits"; and (3) it is "actuated, at least in part, by a purpose to serve the master" (§228).

The scope of employment issue was addressed in *Miller v. CP Chemicals, Inc.* (D.S.C. 1992). Miller, who was an hourly employee, worked mostly from home on his own time. He created computer programs that simplified his duties as laboratory supervisor and decreased the chance of error in the laboratory. Miller's supervisor asked him to create computer programs for other products, which he did. When Miller was terminated from his positions, he asked that CP return his programs or pay a licensing fee for their continued use. CP did not comply and Miller sued CP. The federal court found that Miller had acted within the scope of his employment because he: (1) "was hired primarily for the development of computer programs ... he was responsible for the organization and updating of the laboratory" and that "the development of the computer program was at least incidental to his job responsibilities because it was 'within the ultimate objective of the principal and an act which is not unlikely that such a servant might do"; (2) even though Miller worked from home and was not paid any additional amount for the programs, the work "was performed during the time period in which he was employed by CP"; and (3) the development of the computer programs "was actuated, at least in part, by a purpose to serve the master" (*Miller v. CP Chemicals, Inc.*, D.S.C. 1992, p. 1238). Thus, the court held that the computer programs were created within Miller's scope of employment.

Similarly, in *Marshall v. Miles Laboratories, Inc.* (N.D. Ind. 1986) the employee, Marshall, argued that he had written an article at home, without any instructions from the employer, and did not receive any additional compensation for writing the article. The employer disagreed and stated that Marshall discussed the article with another employee, who is a coauthor of the article, and received funding to present the article at a symposium. In this case, the federal court held that the article was written within the scope of Marshall's employment and that the employer owned the copyright (*Marshall v. Miles Laboratories, Inc.*, N.D. Ind. 1986).

Even though faculty work at home and at their office (prepare for class and conduct scholarly research), given the line of reasoning in Miller and Marshall, it appears that courts will find faculty's work is done within the scope of their employment to serve the master, and thus ownership vests with postsecondary institutions. However, courts may consider the "teacher exception" as an exception to work-for-hire doctrine.

Teacher Exception.   Teacher exception (sometimes referred to as academic exception) exists under common law as an exception to work-for-hire. When courts take this exception into consideration and when it is applied, it vests ownership in the employee rather than employer. Even though some courts have supported the teacher exception under academic tradition, most courts and commentators believe that the teacher exception no longer exists, especially after the passage of the Copyright Act of 1976 and the Supreme Court decision in *CCNV v. Reid* (1989). Two additional cases from 1980s are illustrative of this argument.

In *Weinstein v. University of Illinois* (7th Cir. 1987), faculty members argued over the order of authorship of a published article. Weinstein argued that he was deprived of his due process rights, and the university claimed that Weinstein lacked a property interest in the article. Judge Easterbrook joined by Judge Posner wrote the opinion and held that under the university policy Weinstein had ownership of the article. The court relied on academic tradition and asserted that work-for-hire rules are "general enough to make every academic article a 'work for hire' and therefor vest exclusive control in universities rather than scholars, [but it] has been the academic tradition since copyright law began" that faculty own rights to their own scholarly work (*Weinstein v. University of Illinois*, 7th Cir. 1987, p. 1091).

In *Hays v. Sony Corp. of America* (7th Cir. 1988), two teachers prepared a manual for their students and colleagues on how to use the school's word processors. Two years later, they discovered that Sony had published a manual near identical to theirs, at times a verbatim copy. The teachers sued for copyright infringement. The trial court dismissed the case for failure to state a claim. The Seventh Circuit did not rule on the lower court's dismissal of the case, because the plaintiffs failed to state a claim, but using policy Judge Posner declared his support for the teacher exception. He asserted that prior to 1976 "the universal assumption and practice was that ... the right to copyright such writing belonged to the teacher rather than to the college or university" (*Hays v. Sony Corp. of America*, 7th Cir. 1988, p. 416). Judge Posner's comments were not related to the facts of this case and are considered nonbinding dicta. These two cases provide no specific legal protection for faculty, but tradition and custom may help in asserting the teacher exception. However, while institutional tradition and custom is a long-standing practice in postsecondary institutions, it is not well documented or codified. But if institutional policy is clearly written, it can override claims of institutional tradition and custom.

NEW DIRECTIONS FOR HIGHER EDUCATION • DOI: 10.1002/he

Institutional Policy. In 1999, the American Association of University Professors (AAUP) adopted a policy regarding faculty copyright ownership that includes distance education. The policy states:

> ... it has been the prevailing academic practice to treat the faculty member as the copyright owner of works that are created independently and at the faculty member's own initiative for traditional academic purposes. Examples include class notes and syllabi; books and articles; works of fiction and nonfiction; poems and dramatic works; musical and choreographic works; pictorial, graphic, and sculptural works; and educational software, commonly known as "courseware." This practice has been followed for the most part, regardless of the physical medium in which these "traditional academic works" appear; that is, whether on paper or in audiovisual or electronic form ... this practice should therefore ordinarily apply to the development of courseware for use in programs of distance education. (AAUP, 1999)

According to AAUP guidelines faculty own course materials that they create independently, but recently, most colleges and universities have adopted and published written policies regarding copyright and ownership that may be contrary to the AAUP guidelines. The policies vary significantly among institutions of higher education. Faculty members and other university staff are generally bound by the university policies either through an employment agreement signed when they are hired or through an agreement to comply with the policies set forth in the faculty and staff handbook. For example, the University of Southern California's (USC) courseware policy states:

> In the USC policy, "courseware" is defined as "course syllabi, the expressive content of digital teaching media, CD-ROMs, courses delivered by television, video, Internet or other media or technologies not yet developed, web publications, and any other materials created for the purposes of teaching or instruction or to support the teaching of a course." As set forth in USC's policy, courseware is generally owned by the faculty member who created it unless there is a sponsored research agreement or other controlling agreement to the contrary. (https://policy.usc.edu/courseware/)

The definition and ownership of courseware in this policy clearly includes courses offered via Internet and technologies not yet developed vesting ownership in the faculty, "unless there is a sponsored research agreement or other controlling agreement to the contrary" (https://policy.usc.edu/courseware/). Based on case law, postsecondary institutions generally view faculty as employees and their work as work-for-hire, and most distance learning courses are considered work-for-hire and are within the scope of employment duties. Thus, most institutions will assert ownership for commercial purposes of distance learning courses

New Directions for Higher Education • DOI: 10.1002/he

(Twigg, 2000). However, "course development time, academic freedom, and compensation for these labor-intensive courses will continue to be an issue" (Schifter, 2004; Zhang & Carr-Chellman, 2006).

Traditional and Distance Education

Distance education has the potential to meet the needs of students who cannot afford to be on campus or for nontraditional students who have full-time jobs and/or children. Additionally, distance education is an area that can generate a lot of money for postsecondary institutions (Packard, 2002).

Traditional course materials put on blackboard or faculty-created websites where faculty include syllabi, articles, rubrics, instructions, forum posts, chat rooms, discussion forums are considered faculty owned. The faculty is not asked by the university to create and post these materials, but the faculty member creates and makes these materials available for the students. Thus, these materials and their creation do not fall under the work-for-hire doctrine or the scope of employment. If, however, the university owns its own Internet server, which most postsecondary institutions do, and faculty members use it to create and post these materials, this act brings faculty members' actions closer to work-for-hire (Packard, 2002).

If a faculty member takes their on-the-ground course content and adapts it to an online platform, course ownership is then vested in the institutions via work-for-hire and falls within the scope of employment. Moreover, if the faculty member is compensated for the course by course release, stipend, or course assistants, not only does the faculty member lose ownership of the course, they also do not receive any royalties that are generated through offering the course on mass bases (Packard, 2002). If the institution has substantially contributed to the creation of the online course, ownership is deemed to vest in the intuition. Substantial contribution is defined as support that is in addition to what faculty normally receive, that is, assistance with creating the course, producers hired to create videos used in the course, technical support, course designers (Packard, 2002). Postsecondary institutions' substantial contribution is also defined as a "greater than trivial" contribution by the institution.

When addressing courseware ownership "'greater than trivial' can be defined as 'greater than customary' resources required for a traditional class" (Donohue & Howe-Steiger, 2005, p. 28). Postsecondary institutions' customary contribution to faculty members in traditional classroom-based courses consist of classroom, offices, seat/desks, chalkboard, overhead projector, and library (Donohue & Howe-Steiger, 2005). Courses are stand-alone where the university allows a faculty member to teach it, thus the faculty member has no right to a particular course. Once a faculty member starts to develop the course's products, such as, syllabus, handouts, video clips, power points, readings, lecture notes, web links, and grading rubrics, the faculty member owns the course, because the faculty member provides and uses intellectual and area expertise in creating the course and its products. At this stage, whether the course is offered face-to-face or online by the faculty member who created the course does not matter (Kelley, 2000, October; Porter, 2013).

Issues may arise when the university wants to offer the course online as a MOOC or even have other faculty teach the course as is, without modification, and at times hire adjuncts to teach the course. From the faculty's perspective, there are concerns, such as issues of ownership and academic freedom of the faculty member who created the products. After all, the faculty member independently created the course and used her or his area expertise to create the products for the course, which fall under the Copyright Act as providing original contribution that is greater than trivial. However, the university can make two arguments: (1) that the faculty member is an employee of the institution; and (2) that this work that the faculty member has put into the course is within the scope of his or her employment, and thus the university is vested with ownership of the course.

From the university's perspective, the course belongs to the university and it can control how the course is offered and taught. The faculty member is part of a team and not the only individual making a significant contribution to the final product. The greater than customary contribution of the university to a digital course project might include "instructional designers, information technology specialists, graphic artists; students to test, debug, critique, or refine e-learning courseware; provisions and maintenance of networks, special equipment, software or software licenses; or special media classrooms staffed by specialists in video capture and simulations" (Donohue & Howe-Steiger, 2005, p. 28). Additionally, greater than customary contribution of the institution also includes the university's name or logo; attorneys who handle contracts, licensing agreements, and enforcing copyright registration; marketing of the courses or programs; personnel that oversee financing and investment in this venture (Donohue & Howe-Steiger, 2005). Thus, the amount and use of university resources—substantial use—gives the university the right to own the course and offer it through any means, including MOOCs.

Massive Open Online Courses

MOOCs are increasingly the highlight of education technology, providing open access to educational courses online. More specifically, interactive MOOCs are called connectivist Massive Open Online Course (cMOOC). MOOCs that act as banks of resources without live interaction are called xMOOC. The materials provided in xMOOCs are designed for the masses. Enrollments in MOOCs have reached more than 100,000 students for a single class in some instances (Pappano, 2012). Commonly, xMOOCs are considered less desirable than cMOOCs because the value of higher education is not just the factual content but the social exchange and interaction (Porter, 2013). In this sense, education is a service provided by universities, online and in-person that includes the entire learning environment and the delivery of faculty instruction. Advocates argue that xMOOCs can assist students by offering greater flexibility in course-taking opportunities and save institutional costs by reducing the number of courses a university needs to offer (Berdan, Rhoads, Sayil, & Toven-Lindsey, 2015).

MOOCs and the uses of technology in distance education are evolving much faster than law and institutional policy. Porter (2013) posited that when universities like Harvard, MIT, and UC Berkeley allocate tens of thousands of dollars into developing MOOCs, and providing course releases to faculty members to develop MOOCs, they are certainly going to expect remuneration. They do not, however, want to stifle faculty incentives to author content or lose their best faculty to universities with more faculty-friendly copyright policies. According to Porter:

> The reason most commonly cited for the academic exception to the work-for-hire provision of copyright is academic freedom, but the more pragmatic reasons might well be (1) to promote and reward innovation and excellence, in research as well as teaching, and (2) to retain excellent faculty. One method traditionally used by universities to attract and keep the best faculty and to incentivize their innovation and excellence in teaching and in research, is to allow faculty to retain the copyrights for the works they produce. (2013)

However, faculty ownership of courses is problematic because a course is typically a collection of copyrighted and uncopyrighted materials from a variety of sources. Much of the copyrighted materials is used under the fair use doctrine that allows third-party use of these materials for educational purposes. In the digital age, "the original work of authorship" in intellectual property law is an ambiguous foundational concept (Porter, 2013). Ownership of copyright is accompanied by a bundle of rights—including use, reproduction, and distribution—which can be unbundled (Burk, 1998) through an agreement that recognizes the copyright interests of multiple parties (Klein, 2005). For example, MIT's MOOCs allow faculty members to hold the copyright to their content and provides MIT the rights to distribute the content (Klein, 2005). However, issues arise when faculty assert their right to owning, using, and disseminating traditional course material through various pathways, such as online, to private publishing companies, or other universities as canned MOOC courses.

Legal and Practical Implications for Faculty

Most universities have clear policies "describing how royalties and ownership rights" work and how they are shared among faculty, department, and the institution (Donohue & Howe-Steiger, 2005, p. 24). Established legal precedent shows ownership rights of faculty to traditional courses and lectures they create and present. In the digital world, however, developing a course is a complex endeavor. Unless specific agreements are in place, faculty members who develop and teach online courses may not own the courseware. Most digital courses are created by a team of experts, including the faculty member as the content experts, instructional design experts, and technical experts. These projects also require more than ordinary resources from the university. This substantial use of university resources allows the university to assert ownership over courses created by faculty. The substantial use of university resources are viewed as an investment in courseware, similar to the investments universities make to obtain a patent. Generally, "faculty do not own patents, they receive royalties instead. From an institutional perspective, the same agreement applies in the case of courseware" (Kelley, 2000, October, p. 8–9).

Technology and distance education has developed faster than the laws that regulate them, and the specifics of ownership concerning online courses are not yet clear barring specific agreements with faculty like MOOCs that are offered by various postsecondary institutions, the particulars of online course ownership are not yet clear. The shift from traditional classroom to online teaching implies more than just a change of venue. During this transition, there are several legal and practical implications for faculty, including: (a) decreased number of tenured and tenure track faculty; (b) little changes in tenure structures to accommodate distance course development; (c) an increased number of adjunct and part-time faculty; and (d) increased pressure on faculty to create, develop, and teach online courses without compensation, time off, or other incentives. This could also open the university to legal liability when the "employee," the faculty member, is not compensated in any way (Talab, 2007). That is, the faculty do not receive any course releases, stipend, or graduate students to assist with the creation, development, or teaching of online courses.

Conclusion

Ownership of traditional courseware is vested in the faculty, in the digital forum however, this may not be the case. Agency law's work-for-hire doctrine, Reid's definition of employee–employer relationship and scope of employment, and institutional policy make it clear that ownership of digital courseware is vested in postsecondary institutions. This is especially true if the institution has invested substantial resources in the creation of the digital course. It remains to be seen whether these laws will be revised to protect intellectual property in all modes of delivery for academics, or whether creativity and innovation will depart from the university setting to a business setting? Additionally, if not at the courtroom, where will faculty voice their concerns and how will they protect themselves?

New Directions for Higher Education • DOI: 10.1002/he

References

Abernethy v. Hutchinson, 3 L. J., CH 209, 1 H. T. 28 (1825).

American Association of University Professors. (1999). *Intellectual property issues for faculty*. Retrieved from http://www.aaup.org/issues/copyright-distance-education-intellectual-property/resources-copyright-distance-education-and/intellectual-property-issues-faculty

Aymes v. Bonelli, 980 F.2d 857 (1992).

Berdan Lozano, J., Rhoads, R. A., Sayil Camacho, M., & Toven-Lindsey, B. (2015). The massive open online course movement, xMOOCs, and faculty labor. *The Review of Higher Education, 38*(3), 407–408.

Bleistein v. Donaldson Lithographing Company, 188 U.S. 239 (1903).

Burk, D. L. (1998). Ownership of electronic course materials in higher education. *Campus-Wide Information Systems, 15*(4), 142–147.

Colliery Engineer Co. v. United Correspondence Schools Co., 94 F. 152 (C.C.D. N.Y. 1899).

Community for Creative Non-Violence v. Reid, 490 U.S. at 730 (1989).

Daniel, P. T. K., & Pauken, P. D. (2015). Intellectual property in higher education. In R. Fossey & S. Eckes (Eds.), *Contemporary issues in higher education law* (3rd ed.). Cleveland, OH: Education Law Association.

Donohue, B. C., & Howe-Steiger, L. (2005). Faculty and administrators collaborating for e-learning courseware; faculty incentives, clear ownership and usage rights, and adequate funding will encourage faculty to explore technology for teaching. *EDUCAUSE Quarterly, 28*(1), 20–32.

Feist Publ'ns, Inc. v. Rural Telephone Services Company, 499 U.S. 340, 345 (1991).

Hays v. Sony Corp. of America, 847 F.2d 412, 416 (7th Cir. 1988).

Kelley, K. B. (2000, October). Courseware Development for Distance Education: Issues and Policy Models for Faculty Ownership. For full text: http://www.educause.edu/conference/e2000/proceedings.html. For full text: http://www.educause.edu/asp/doclib/abstract.asp?ID=EDU0015.html

Klein, M. W. (2005). Protecting faculty rights in copyright ownership policies. 21st Annual Conference on Distance Teaching and Learning. Retrieved from http://www.uwex.edu/disted/conference/Resource_library/search_detail.cfm?presid=2046

Laughlin, G. (2000). Who owns the copyright to faculty-created web sites? The work-for-hire doctrine's applicability to internet resources created for distance learning and traditional classroom courses. 41 *B.C.L. Rev* 549.

Marshall v. Miles Laboratories, Inc., 647 F. Supp. 1326 (N.D. Ind. 1986).

Miller v. CP Chemicals, Inc. 808 F. Supp. at 1238 (D.S.C. 1992).

Packard, A. (2002). Copyright or copy wrong: An analysis of university claims to faculty work. *7 Communication Law & Policy*, 275.

Pappano, L. (2012). The year of the MOOC. *New York Times*. Retrieved from http://www.nytimes.com

Porter, J. E. (2013). The CCCC-IP Annual: Top intellectual property developments of 2012. Available from the Intellectual Property Caucus of the Conference on College Composition and Communication.

Priest, D. (2012). Copyright and the Harvard Open Access Mandate. *Northwestern Journal of Technology and Intellectual Property*, 10 Nw. J. Tech. & Intell. Prop. 377.

Restatement Second of Agency §228 (1958).

Schifter, C. (2004). Compensation Models in Distance Education: National Survey Questionnaire Revisited. *Online Journal of Distance Learning Administration*, 7(1).

Talab, R. (2007). Copyright and you: Faculty distance courseware ownership and the "Wal-Mart" approach to higher education. *TechTrends*, 51(4).

Twigg, C. A. (2000). Who owns online courses and course materials. *Intellectual property policies for a new learning environment*.

U.S. Const. art. I, §8 (1787).

U.S. Copyright Act of 1909, Pub.L. 60–349, 35 Stat. 1075, H.R. 28192, enacted March 4 (1909).

U.S. Copyright Act, 17 USC §201 (1976).

University of Southern California, Policy Courseware. Retrieved from https://policy.usc.edu/courseware/

Weinstein v. University of Illinois, 811 F.2d 1091 (7th Cir. 1987).

Williams v. Weisser, 273 C.A. 2d 726, 78 Cal. Rptr. 542 (1969).

Zhang, K., & Carr-Chellman, A. (2006). Courseware copyright: Whose rights are right? *Journal of Educational Computing Research*, 34(2), 173–186.

SHAFIQA AHMADI is an associate professor of clinical education at the Rossier School of Education. Her research focuses on diversity and legal protection of underrepresented students, and her teaching focuses on legal issues in higher education administration. She received her doctor of jurisprudence from Indiana University School of Law, at Bloomington, Indiana.

New Directions for Higher Education • DOI: 10.1002/he

3

This chapter provides a history of the scholarly publishing system, and explains how it has evolved to benefit corporate publishers to the detriment of faculty, universities, and the public. It offers the open access movement as a potential remedy for the publishing crisis, and the policy environment surrounding these new forms of communication.

Faculty Rights to Scholarly Research

Molly Kleinman

The publication of peer-reviewed research is one of the cornerstones of scholarly work (Blackburn & Lawrence, 1995). Throughout academia, faculty must publish their research in order to participate in the "Great Conversation" of scholarship, which occurs across space and time and includes their living peers, as well as with the researchers that came before and those that will come after (Guédon, 2014). The basic forms in which researchers communicate their findings to colleagues—peer-reviewed journal articles and monographs—have remained largely unchanged over the past century, even though the economics of the system changed dramatically with the rise of the Internet (T. C. Bergstrom, 2001).

For better or worse, the design of copyright law, the legal system that governs the scholarly publishing system, and by extension, the Great Conversation does not consider the norms and needs of academics (Willinsky, 2002). Meanwhile, control over most scholarly work, in the form of copyright ownership, has migrated from scholars and nonprofit journals into the hands of a few large publishing corporations. There is research to suggest that this has resulted in reduced access to scholarship even for researchers at the wealthiest institutions, causing what has become known as "the scholarly communications crisis" (C. T. Bergstrom & Bergstrom, 2006; Yiotis, 2005).

As awareness of the flaws in the existing system has grown, some faculty members have begun attempting to retain their copyrights and provide broader access to their work, by renegotiating terms with established publishers, organizing to implement institutional policies in favor of faculty rights, or circumventing conventional paths to publication in favor of online open access journals. These approaches offer a number of advantages, such as allowing faculty members to maintain control of their copyrights,

NEW DIRECTIONS FOR HIGHER EDUCATION, no. 177, Spring 2017 © 2017 Wiley Periodicals, Inc.
Published online in Wiley Online Library (wileyonlinelibrary.com) • DOI: 10.1002/he.20224

promoting greater visibility for research, and improving public access to scholarship. These shifts in the management of faculty rights to scholarly research have produced a new politics of scholarly publishing, one that has proven to be surprisingly controversial.

This chapter provides a basic overview of recent changes in both rules governing scholarly copyright, the economics of scholarly publishing, and an introduction to the open access movement, along with its various attempts to help faculty and universities regain control of their academic publications.

Brief Copyright Overview

Faculty rights to scholarly research are governed by layers of institutional policy, federal law, and social convention. Several surveys have suggested that most faculty possess a very limited understanding of copyright laws and policies, and misconceptions about it persist across disciplines and institution types (Rowlands, Nicholas, & Huntingdon, 2004; Sims, 2011). Therefore, in order to discuss some of the intricacies of the system, it helps to begin with a very brief review of the basics. These basic facts provide a snapshot of both the strengths and weaknesses in the current copyright system as it applies to academic research.

The Purpose of Copyright.   The Constitutional purpose of copyright is to promote the progress of science and art (U.S. Const. art. 1, §8, cl. 8). Its original purpose was not for the government to provide incentives to creators, offer rewards for hard work, or enable complete control over a given creation. The authors of early copyright law believed that creators and inventors did not require incentives; they would create and invent regardless of the surrounding legal regime (Boyle, 2008). Recent debates about copyright law and policy often focus on incentives and control, but the intellectual property clause in the U.S. Constitution, and indeed copyright law itself for the first 200 years, sought a balance between the needs of the public to benefit from creative work and the needs of the creator to reap some reward from her or his work (Litman, 2001). This balancing between public and private interests is intrinsic to most kinds of academic labor, from teaching to research, and scholarly publishing was once no different (Kezar, 2004). In the past few decades, copyright laws have shifted strongly in favor of private ownership interests over the needs and desires of the public, raising challenges for creators whose copyrights are unlikely to earn them millions of dollars, which is to say, the vast majority of people who have ever assembled a syllabus or written an email.

Where Copyright Comes From and How Long it Lasts.   Copyright happens automatically the moment a work is created, and in most cases, it lasts for the entire lifetime of the creator, plus an additional 70 years after the creator has died (Leaffer, 2010). For a journal article by a 45-year-old mid-career scholar who lives to the entirely plausible age of 85, that would

NEW DIRECTIONS FOR HIGHER EDUCATION • DOI: 10.1002/he

be a 110-year copyright term. Few academics realize that they hold copyrights in nearly all of their creations, from published articles to syllabi to listserv emails, or that these rights will persist long after they die (Sims, 2011).

Like the emphasis on "incentives" that dominates the present copyright debates, this automatic and lengthy enclosure happened only recently. Prior to 1978, the law required creators or publishers to register their works with the U.S. Copyright Office in order to gain copyright protection. Unregistered works entered immediately into the public domain, which meant that anyone could use the works for any reason, without paying a license fee and without the permission of the creator (Boyle, 2008). Until 1989, protection also required proper notice of copyright protection, in the form of the familiar © symbol and the year of publication; lack of proper notice was sufficient for a work to enter the public domain (Smith, 2014).

Furthermore, the duration of the first copyrights lasted for 14 years, with the option to renew for another 14 years. After the term expired, those works also entered the public domain (Leaffer, 2010). In the past 40 years, Congress has extended copyright terms 11 times, thanks mostly to intensive lobbying efforts by the entertainment industry (Lessig, 2004). Because those repeated term extensions came just as a new wave of older works were about to enter the public domain, we have entered a period in which copyright terms are "the functional equivalent of perpetual," and very few older works become available for free public reuse (Eric Eldred et al., *Petitioners v. John D. Ashcroft*, Attorney General, 2003, Stevens, J., dissenting, p. 21).

Rights Associated With Copyright.   Copyright is a set of five limited rights. It includes the rights to reproduce, distribute, prepare derivative works such as translations or film adaptations, perform, and display a given work (17 U.S.C. §106). Within the scope of those limited rights, copyright holders essentially have a monopoly on the use of a particular work. Copyright holders can transfer those rights in a single bundle, or license some rights while retaining others (Leaffer, 2010). In scholarly publishing, the tradition has generally been that authors transfer the entire bundle of rights over to publishers, often for free (Smith, 2014). Many academic authors do not realize that once they sign the contract, or check the "accept" box on the web form, they no longer have the right to additional uses of their work such as translations, reprinting in an anthology, or even posting the articles online, to a personal website or a repository like the Social Science Research Network (Rowlands et al., 2004).

This divisibility of copyright into separate rights can be of great benefit to academics who want to preserve their own rights and the rights of others to use and build upon their work. It means an author can grant a nonexclusive license to a journal to publish an article, while simultaneously retaining the right to post it on his or her website, permit colleagues to distribute it in course packs, or even allow translations. Although this rarely happens in practice, the potential to unbundle copyrights, keeping some rights while giving away others, enables the changes currently happening across the scholarly publishing system.

The Changing Economics of Scholarly Publishing

Eternal, automatic, and monopolistic copyright protection may have value for the owners of Mickey Mouse, but in an academic context, it has proven highly problematic, clashing both with traditional approaches to managing ownership of scholarly work, and with the freedom and flexibility inherent in the networked age (Benkler, 2006). In the days of print, making and distributing copies of scholarly articles was expensive. Most journal publishers were scholarly societies and university presses that earned little in the way of profits, often while receiving subsidies from parent institutions (Velterop, 2003). Journals managed copyright licensing on behalf of authors, and in return, authors transferred copyrights for free, with the confidence that the journal was the best possible mechanism to provide broad access to their published articles (Smith, 2014).

However, starting in the 1980s with the early days of the Internet and rise of electronic journals and databases, the economics of scholarly publishing changed dramatically. A few big corporate publishers started buying the rights to publish and distribute large numbers of scholarly journals, and learned that especially in the STEM fields, they could charge high access fees to businesses and universities for access to those journals (Montgomery & Sparks, 2000). Authors continued transferring their copyrights to publishers for free, but now publishers were earning increasingly large profits for that free labor, and had become principally committed to shareholder profits instead of the scholarly community (T. C. Bergstrom, 2001).

An outcome of the industry-wide change in ownership is that the cost of access to scholarly journals has risen at roughly four times the cost of inflation for over the past 30 years (Kyrillidou, Morris, & Roebuck, 2013). It has also had disastrous effects on access to academic journals. One important study found that comparing both price per page and price per recent citation, for-profit journal subscriptions cost 5 times as much as nonprofit journals in the same field (C. T. Bergstrom & Bergstrom, 2006). This is true even when controlling for the quality of the journal, using citation rates as a proxy.

The authors go on to demonstrate that high prices lead to decreased access, because a journal's circulation is closely connected to its price. The higher the cost of a journal, the fewer libraries subscribe to it, and therefore fewer scholars are able to access it through their institutional affiliations. However, faculty remain largely unaware of these inefficiencies, and continue to publish in expensive, for-profit journals, likely because that is where their colleagues publish, and also what their colleagues read. In short, even though for-profit journals are incurring significant strain on the scholarly communication system as a whole by increasing costs and limiting access, there have been few incentives for faculty to change their publishing behavior (Schonfeld & Housewright, 2010).

This difference in the costs of for-profit and nonprofit journals highlights the disconnect between the practices of the old scholarly publishing system, which was run by and for scholars, and the economic realities of the new scholarly publishing system, run largely by corporations and for the benefit of shareholders. Under the old system, it was accepted that much of the labor was uncompensated, in part because after the expenses of printing, binding, and shipping journal issues, there was very little money to go around (Givler, 2002). Publishers did not pay scholars for the articles they wrote, or for the time they spent peer reviewing others' articles. Instead, the benefits of publishing accrued to scholars in other ways, largely through the tenure and promotion system.

Today's for-profit publishers benefit from the free writing and reviewing customs of the old system, in an environment where the Internet has reduced the marginal cost of making and distributing a copy to zero (Benkler, 2006). Although managing peer review and maintaining online article databases are not free, those expenses do not come close to explaining the astronomical rise in subscription fees. Rather, the maintenance of publishers' marketing departments, sales forces, executive salaries, and positive annual profit reports consumes those excess dollars, none of which benefit the scholarly community that sustains them (C. T. Bergstrom & Bergstrom, 2006).

This system squeezes faculty from all sides. As researchers, many struggle to access relevant articles because university libraries have spent the past 20 years cutting journal subscriptions in the face of flat or declining budgets and rising prices (Bosch & Henderson, 2013). The increase in journal costs has even encroached on monograph budgets; reduced book buying has so damaged university presses that many have shuttered, while many more have attempted to shift their focus toward books with more commercial appeal (Sherman, 2014). This drop in academic book publishing has disproportionately affected faculty authors in the humanities, who find it harder to publish the monographs required for tenure, just as the competition for tenure-track positions has risen (Townsend, 2003). Faculty continue to write and review for free, even though the benefits of tenure and promotion are becoming harder to achieve.

For-profit scholarly publishing has permanently altered the ecosystem of scholarly communication, reducing access to published work on the one hand, while constraining opportunities to publish on the other. In response, a growing assortment of faculty, administrators, funders, librarians, patient advocates, and policy makers have been taking action to bring the system back into balance.

NEW DIRECTIONS FOR HIGHER EDUCATION • DOI: 10.1002/he

Retaining Rights to Expand Access

Although technology transfer offices to manage faculty-produced patents have been around for decades, most universities have taken a hands-off approach to copyrights in scholarly research (Slaughter & Rhoades, 2010). Formal policies and informal customs permitted faculty to retain control over their copyrights, which in practice meant that most faculty promptly gave up control of their copyrights the moment the opportunity to publish arose. Likewise, government agencies and foundations rarely asserted any rights in the peer-reviewed articles resulting from their funding. As awareness of the crisis in scholarly communication has grown, a range of responses has sprung up, from the individual level, to institutional and federal policies, all seeking to assert more control over faculty articles in order to limit publisher monopolies and improve future access.

The Open Access Movement.   The main impetus for these policies arose from the open access movement, which defines acceptable levels of free access to scholarly literature, as well as promoting paths to achieve that access (Suber, 2012). The open access movement advocates for free, online access to peer reviewed scholarship. It is grounded in two basic arguments: (1) the Internet makes possible free and instantaneous distribution of knowledge, and so academia should avail itself of the efficiencies afforded by the network; and (2) the scholarly communication system is broken; faculty write scholarly articles for free, based on research that was often funded by taxpayers, and those articles should be freely available to the public (Wellen, 2004; Willinsky, 2002).

The movement has coalesced around two ways for a work to be open access: self-archiving and open access publishing. With self-archiving, the author publishes an article in a traditional journal and posts a copy on a publicly available online repository or website. Self-archiving has the advantage of permitting faculty to continue publishing in whichever journals they choose, while enabling broader access to their work, and it is the path that most institutional and governmental policies have taken. It is an option for all scholars, regardless of discipline, as long as they have access to the Internet.

In open access publishing, an author chooses to publish in one of the growing number of open access journals, which are made freely available online from the moment of publication (Bailey, 2006). Open access journals serve as direct competition for traditional for-profit publishers, but a respected open access journal must exist in the author's field in order for open access publishing to be a viable option (Park & Qin, 2007). Many open access journals charge a fee for publication as a replacement for subscription income; while some grant funders are beginning to cover those costs, access to money to pay publication fees vary widely by discipline (Solomon & Björk, 2012). There are some established, high-impact open access journals, particularly in the sciences, but it has taken time for them to build their reputations (Tenopir et al., 2013).

Both self-archiving and open access publishing are relatively young concepts, only as old as the Internet. It has experienced rapid growth in the past 15 years, as the web has become more widely available and network speeds have increased (Suber, 2012). As a result, the study of open access practices among faculty is quite new, and methodologies and conceptual frameworks for understanding them are still nascent. We know that open access publishing has grown tremendously, and that open access appears to increase an article's download and citation rates, but we do not know yet why some high-quality open access journals succeed while others do not (Davis, Lewenstein, Simon, Booth, & Connolly, 2008; Gargouri et al., 2010; Laakso et al., 2011). Researchers are just starting to uncover the incentives and influences affecting faculty self-archiving and open access publishing behavior (e.g., Kim, 2010; Park & Qin, 2007; Xia, 2011), let alone a comprehensive understanding of what impact the open access movement is having on the scholarly communications system as a whole.

Open Access Mandates.   One clear trend that has arisen from the open access movement is the proliferation of open access mandates (Joseph, 2008; Suber, 2012). Universities, research institutes, and funding bodies have begun to require that faculty make their published research freely available online, usually through some version of self-archiving, often after an embargo period of 6 months to a year, during which publishers preserve a temporary monopoly on the right to sell access to the work. By placing this requirement on faculty before they sign their copyrights over to publishers, mandates circumvent any need to negotiate for these rights on a case-by-case basis.

Many universities offer their own archive services, called institutional repositories, where faculty can deposit all of their published work (Shreeves & Cragin, 2008). Some funders are following suit, including the NIH and the Bill and Melinda Gates Foundation (Bill & Melinda Gates Foundation, 2014; NIH, 2008). The National Institutes of Health (NIH) Public Access Policy enacted in 2008 requires that all peer reviewed articles resulting from NIH funding be made freely available in the PubMed Central online repository within 12 months of publication (NIH, 2008). The Gates Foundation requires that both published articles and underlying data be freely available online; it currently permits an embargo, but will require immediate free access beginning in 2017.

University open access mandates generally emerge from faculty senates or other self-governing bodies. Rather than top-down policies imposed by administrators, institutional open access mandates appear to arise from a growing awareness among the faculty themselves that the scholarly publishing system is not working for them anymore (Suber, 2010). More than 100 colleges and universities in the United States have now enacted open access mandates, including Harvard, Stanford, and the University of California (Registry of Open Access Repository Mandates and Policies, 2014). These mandates offer a number of advantages for faculty, putting institutional support behind faculty members who wish to maintain control of their copyrights while also promoting greater visibility for their research, and better serving the mission of higher education by improving public access to scholarship (Joseph, 2008).

Despite this burgeoning faculty consensus, funder mandates have met with great controversy, especially at the federal level. Before Congress passed the NIH policy in 2008, the Association for American Publishers (AAP) argued that the policy would kill the subscription revenues of for-profit scientific publishers, rendering them unable to recoup the costs of publication (PRISM Coalition, 2007). Members of Congress have made multiple attempts to pass legislation, such as Federal Research Public Access Act (FRPAA) and the Fair Access to Science and Technology Research Act (FASTR), which would expand the NIH Policy to include several of the largest federal funding agencies, but the AAP has led opposition to these bills as well, and as yet none have left committee.

The AAP argues that mandating free access to publicly funded research would violate publishers' copyrights, destroy the peer-review system, and decimate the for-profit publishing industry (Adler & Frank, 2012; Howard, 2012; Sporkin, 2011). While evidence to support these assertions is scant, they have thus far been successful in staving off further attempts to enshrine open access in the law. In 2013, the Office of Science and Technology Policy released a memorandum requiring Federal agencies with more than $100 million in research and development expenditures to devise plans to implement public access policies similar to the NIH. At present, there is no process in place to implement these plans (Stebbins, 2013). However, for-profit publishers are clearly feeling the pressure to offer more open publishing models. Companies like Springer and Elsevier have started offering "open choice" options, which aim to split the difference between traditional publishing and open access. Authors may publish in their traditional journals and pay a fee, usually in the range of $2,500 to $3,000, for the publisher to make the article freely available from the moment of publication (e.g., Elsevier, 2015; Springer, n.d.). The questions of who should pay for this fee, and whether it accurately reflects the revenue that the publisher loses by making the article freely available online, remain unresolved.

Looking Ahead

The advancement of the open access movement in recent years is a promising sign that the crisis in scholarly communication may one day end. Peer-reviewed articles are how scholars communicate with each other across space and time, they tell researchers what has worked and what has not, and

NEW DIRECTIONS FOR HIGHER EDUCATION • DOI: 10.1002/he

they document what we as a society know and what we are still learning. And they are becoming so expensive that even Harvard can no longer afford their subscriptions (Rosen, 2012). Diminished access to published scholarship threatens the public service mission of higher education by keeping the results of research locked away in subscription journals to which few have access.

Open access publishing, open access mandates, and author self-archiving have the potential to bring scholarly publishing back into alignment with the mission and goals of academia. Journals that have in recent years provided a profit engine for private corporations may once again serve the individuals and institutions that created them. Democratizing access to the knowledge that universities produce will have benefits far outside the confines of the ivory tower, and provide an opportunity to serve the public in a way that has been largely overlooked in the existing higher education literature on public service.

Indeed, although the study of faculty patent ownership is well established in the field, faculty rights to their publications have been almost entirely overlooked. As the open access movement enters the mainstream and its effects emerge, perhaps there will become a place in the higher education literature for the study of access not just to a college degree, but to the publications that are one of the primary outputs of academic research.

References

Adler, A., & Frank, M. (2012). *Response to the Office of Science and Technology Policy's request for information regarding "Public access to peer-reviewed scholarly publications resulting from federally funded research."* Retrieved from http://www.publishers.org/_attachments/docs/library/01-10-2012%20ostp%20publications%20rfi%20aap-psp%20response%20-%20final.pdf

Bailey, C. W. (2006). What is open access? In N. Jacobs (Ed.), *Open access: Key strategic, technical and economic aspects* (pp. 13–26). Oxford, UK: Chandos.

Benkler, Y. (2006). *The wealth of networks: How social production transforms markets and freedom.* New Haven, CT: Yale University Press.

Bergstrom, C. T., & Bergstrom, T. C. (2006). The economics of ecology journals. *Frontiers in Ecology and the Environment, 4*(9), 488–495.

Bergstrom, T. C. (2001). Free labor for costly journals? *Journal of Economic Perspectives, 15*(4), 183–198. doi:10.1257/jep.15.4.183

Bill & Melinda Gates Foundation. (2014). *Bill & Melinda Gates Foundation open access policy [Web page].* Retrieved from http://www.gatesfoundation.org/how-we-work/general-information/open-access-policyholders

Blackburn, R. T., & Lawrence, J. H. (1995). *Faculty at work: Motivation, expectation, satisfaction.* Baltimore, MD: The Johns Hopkins University Press.

Bosch, S., & Henderson, K. (2013, April 25). The winds of change: Periodicals price survey 2013. *Library Journal.* Retrieved from http://lj.libraryjournal.com/2013/04/publishing/the-winds-of-change-periodicals-price-survey-2013/

Boyle, J. (2008). *The public domain: Enclosing the commons of the mind.* New Haven, CT: Yale University Press.

NEW DIRECTIONS FOR HIGHER EDUCATION • DOI: 10.1002/he

Davis, P. M., Lewenstein, B. V, Simon, D. H., Booth, J. G., & Connolly, M. J. L. (2008). Open access publishing, article downloads, and citations: Randomised controlled trial. *BMJ, 337*, 1–6. doi:10.1136/bmj.a568

Elsevier. (2015). *Open access options* [Web page]. Retrieved from http://www. elsevier.com/about/open-access/open-access-options

Eric Eldred et al. Petitioners v. John D. Ashcroft, Attorney General, US 01–618 (2003). (Stevens, J., dissenting).

Gargouri, Y., Hajjem, C., Larivière, V., Gingras, Y., Carr, L., Brody, T., & Harnad, S. (2010). Self-selected or mandated, open access increases citation impact for higher quality research. *PloS One, 5*(10), e13636. doi:10.1371/journal.pone.0013636

Givler, P. (2002). University press publishing in the United States. In R. E. Able & L. W. Newman (Eds.), *Scholarly publishing: Books, journals, and libraries in the twentieth century*. New York, NY: Wiley.

Guédon, J. C. (2014). Sustaining the "Great Conversation": The future of scholarly and scientific journals. In B. Cope & A. Phillips (Eds.), *The Future of the Academic Journal* pp. (85–112). Oxford, UK: Chandos.

Howard, J. (2012). Who gets to see published research? *The Chronicle of Higher Education*. Retrieved from http://chronicle.com/article/Who-Gets-to-See-Published/130403/

Joseph, H. (2008). A question of access—Evolving policies and practices. *Journal of Library Administration, 48*(1), 95–106.

Kezar, A. J. (2004). Obtaining integrity? Reviewing and examining the charter between higher education and society. *The Review of Higher Education, 27*(4), 429–459. doi:10.1353/rhe.2004.0013

Kim, J. (2010). Faculty self-archiving: Motivations and barriers. *Journal of the American Society for Information Science, 61*(9), 1909–1922. doi:10.1002/asi

Kyrillidou, M., Morris, S., & Roebuck, G. (2013). *ARL Statistics 2011–2012*. Washington, DC: Association of Research Libraries.

Laakso, M., Welling, P., Bukvova, H., Nyman, L., Björk, B.-C., & Hedlund, T. (2011). The development of open access journal publishing from 1993 to 2009. *PloS One, 6*(6), e20961. doi:10.1371/journal.pone.0020961

Leaffer, M. A. (2010). *Understanding copyright law*. New Providence, NJ: LexisNexis.

Lessig, L. (2004). *Free culture: How big media uses technology and the law to lock down culture and control creativity*. New York, NY: Penguin.

Litman, J. (2001). *Digital copyright*. Amherst, NY: Prometheus Books.

Montgomery, C. H., & Sparks, J. L. (2000). The transition to an electronic journal collection: Managing the organizational changes. *Serials Review, 26*(3), 4–18.

NIH Public Access Policy. (2008). Division G, Title II, Section 218 of PL 110–161 (Consolidated Appropriations Act, 2008). Retrieved from http:// publicaccess.nih.gov/policy.htm

Park, J.-hong, & Qin, J. (2007). Exploring the willingness of scholars to accept open access: A grounded theory approach. *Journal of Scholarly Publishing, 38*(2), 55–84.

PRISM Coalition. (2007). *Government legislation & regulation: S 2695 – FRPAA*. Retrieved from http://www.prismcoalition.org/legislation_2695.htm

Registry of Open Access Repository Mandates and Policies. (2014). [Internet database]. Retrieved from http://roarmap.eprints.org/view/country/840.html

Rosen, R. J. (2012). Harvard now spending nearly $3.75 million on academic journal bundles. *The Atlantic*. Retrieved from http://www.theatlantic.com/technology/ archive/2012/04/harvard-now-spending-nearly-375-million-on-academic-journal-bundles/256248/

Rowlands, I., Nicholas, D., & Huntingdon, P. (2004). *Scholarly communication in the digital environment: What do authors want?* [Report]. London, UK: Centre for Information Behaviour and the Evaluation of Research.

Schonfeld, R. C., & Housewright, R. (2010). *Faculty survey 2009: Key strategic insights for libraries, publishers, and societies* [Report]. New York, NY: Ithaka S+R.

Sherman, S. (2014, May 26). University presses under fire. *The Nation*. Retrieved from http://www.thenation.com/article/179712/university-presses-under-fire

Shreeves, S. L., & Cragin, M. H. (2008). Introduction: Institutional repositories: Current state and future. *Library Trends, 57*(2), 89–97. doi:10.1353/lib.0.0037

Sims, N. (2011). Lies, damned lies, and copyright (mis) information: Empowering faculty by addressing key points of confusion. *In Association of College and Research Libraries 2011 Conference Proceedings.*

Slaughter, S., & Rhoades, G. (2010). The social construction of copyright ethics and values. *Science and Engineering Ethics, 16*(2), 263–293. doi:10.1007/s11948-009-9162-1

Smith, K. L. (2014). *Owning and using scholarship: An IP handbook for teachers and researchers.* Chicago, IL: Association of College and Research Libraries.

Solomon, D. J., & Björk, B.-C. (2012). Publication fees in open access publishing: Sources of funding and factors influencing choice of journal. *Journal of the Association for Information Science and Technology, 63,* 98–107. doi:10.1002/asi.21660

Sporkin, A. (2011). *Publishers applaud "Research Works Act," bipartisan legislation to end government mandates on private-sector scholarly publishing* [Press release]. Retrieved from http://www.publishers.org/press/56/

Springer. (n.d.). *Open choice: Your research, your choice* [Web page]. Retrieved from http://www.springer.com/gp/open-access/springer-open-choice

Stebbins, M. (2013). *Expanding public access to the results of federally funded research* [Press release]. Retrieved from http://www.whitehouse.gov/blog/2013/02/22/expanding-public-access-results-federally-funded-research

Suber, P. (2010). Unanimous faculty votes. *SPARC Open Access Newsletter, 146.* Retrieved from http://legacy.earlham.edu/~peters/fos/newsletter/06-02-10.htm#votes

Suber, P. (2012). *Open access.* Cambridge, MA: MIT Press.

Townsend, R. B. (2003, October). History and the future of scholarly publishing. *Perspectives on History.* Retrieved from http://www.historians.org/publications-and-directories/perspectives-on-history/october-2003/history-and-the-future-of-scholarly-publishing

Tenopir, C., Allard, S., Levine, K., Volentine, R., Christian, L., Boehm, R., …Thornley, C. (2013). *Trust and authority in scholarly communications in the light of the digital transition* (p. 76). Retrieved from http://ciber-research.eu/download/20140115-Trust_Final_Report.pdf

U.S. Constitution, Article 1, Section 8, Clause 8.

U.S. Code, Title 17, Section 106.

Velterop, J. (2003). Should scholarly societies embrace open access (or is it the kiss of death)? *Learned Publishing, 16*(3), 167–169.

Wellen, R. (2004). Taking on commercial scholarly journals: Reflections on the "open access" movement. *Journal of Academic Ethics, 2*(1), 101–118. doi:10.1023/B:JAET.0000039010.14325.3d

Willinsky, J. (2002). Copyright contradictions in scholarly publishing. *First Monday, 7*(11–4). Retrieved from http://firstmonday.org/htbin/cgiwrap/bin/ojs/index.php/fm/article/view/1006/927

Xia, J. (2011). Constructing the structure underlying open access practices. *Journal of Information Science, 37*(3), 322–331. doi:10.1177/0165551511404868

Yiotis, K. (2005). The open access initiative: A new paradigm for scholarly communications. *Information technology and libraries, 24*(4), 157–162.

MOLLY KLEINMAN is a doctoral candidate at the University of Michigan, with a concentration in Public Policy in Postsecondary Education. She is also completing a certificate in Science, Technology, and Public Policy at U-M's Ford School of Public Policy. Molly holds a master of science in information (2007) from the University of Michigan, and earned her BA in English (1997) from Bryn Mawr College.

NEW DIRECTIONS FOR HIGHER EDUCATION • DOI: 10.1002/he

4

This chapter explores the theoretical assumptions underlying both the IP system and its counternarrative, academic openness, to encourage stakeholders to look beyond extremes as depicted in political rhetoric, and find a compromise consistent with the common mission of faculty, universities, and publishers.

"Owning" Knowledge: Looking Beyond Politics to Find the Public Good

Samantha Bernstein-Sierra

This chapter provides an introduction to the concept of openness as the antithesis of intellectual property (IP). Rooted in the economic concept of the "commons," openness refers to a kind of transparency. In academic materials such as courseware or research, openness facilitates access, in contrast to IP, which by its nature restricts access to academic materials to allow rights holders to exclude others and profit from those works. In response to the influx of academic capitalist values, "openness" has evolved into a social movement, fueled by advocates who seek to ease restrictions on educational materials for the good of society, and to restore balance to the property regime within the academy. The purpose of this chapter is twofold. First, it aims to educate faculty and administrators about the broader legal and philosophical environment surrounding IP in higher education, and second, it proposes a practical path for faculty to contribute to policy change through openness advocacy.

The chapter first describes the relationship between openness and IP, and the evolution of the openness movement in higher education. Second, it frames openness as a debate between two competing political narratives. The chapter concludes with the practical implications of openness for faculty, universities, and publishers.

Open Commons and Closed Commodities

Universities operate in accordance with the dual and often competing missions of social progress and commercial gain (Hervieux, Gedajlovic, & Turcotte, 2010), which arise out of conflicting ideas about whether higher education is a public or a private good. Although both the public

NEW DIRECTIONS FOR HIGHER EDUCATION, no. 177, Spring 2017 © 2017 Wiley Periodicals, Inc.
Published online in Wiley Online Library (wileyonlinelibrary.com) • DOI: 10.1002/he.20225

and private missions coexist within most campuses and are competing forces, the trend toward greater market-based strategies has impacted how universities perceive the commercial value of their knowledge assets, such as the quality of their courses, the reputation of their faculty members, and the fruits of research (Gumport & Sporn, 1999). Because the ownership and control of information resources is a source of great wealth in the knowledge economy (Thurow, 2000), universities seek to leverage these assets in order to gain a competitive advantage in a market largely dominated by revenue-generation. IP law allows for ownership of knowledge assets, and can be used as a profit-generating mechanism in line with universities' commercial mission.

IP law is defined in contradistinction to the "commons"—a conceptual space where knowledge resides that cannot, or should not, be owned (McSherry, 2009, p. 6). The commons exists beyond capitalist structures like markets and hierarchies and is designated for use and enjoyment by all members of a society (Bollier, 2007). The commons can be tangible or intangible, natural or man-made. Libraries are a commons, as are Wikipedia and the works of Shakespeare (Boyle, 2008, p. 39); their defining feature is that no person can be excluded from using them.

Owning Knowledge.   Knowledge is a commons because it is nonexcludable; with sufficient mental capacity, no person can be excluded from acquiring it (Stiglitz, 1999). Though knowledge in its pure form, as ideas, information, and concepts (Peters, 2003) is nonexcludable, its expression is not. When ideas are expressed in tangible form—as books and musical compositions—those forms can be made excludable and commodified. In order to incentivize authors and musicians to continue to write and compose, governments grant limited monopolies to knowledge creators in the form of IP rights. IP, and specifically copyright, is the legal mechanism that allows creators to exclude others from accessing the book or composition, and ultimately charge a fee for their work. IP transforms common resources into commodities. Viewed in this light, IP represents an "enclosure" of the knowledge commons (Boyle, 2003).

Property rights over knowledge raise important societal questions for governments, rights holders, and the public (Peters, 2003). Expansive IP rights—those that heavily restrict access to the public for the benefit of the copyright or patent holder—signal a danger of market monopolization, while more permissive IP rights risk reducing the knowledge supply by removing incentives for the knowledge producer. Effective IP systems must therefore balance between incentivizing knowledge creation and restricting public access to it (Stiglitz, 1999).

The university has long been assigned the role of gatekeeper of the commons (McSherry, 2009). Academic work, such as research papers, datasets, and courses differs from artistic and literary expression in a number of ways. Unlike artists and authors, academics do not profit directly from the sale of their work. Successful academic careers require that faculty members create, promote, and disseminate their scholarly work, building reputations through attribution: the currency system of the academic profession. Academic research is a cumulative process. In exchange for ideas, faculty members cite original authors, who in turn receive the visibility benefits of those citations. Citations are accumulated and used as evidence of work quality, and ultimately converted into monetary benefits like salary, promotion, and tenure. For these reasons, academics have traditionally consented to relinquish copyright to their work to academic publishers in exchange for publication and dissemination.

One of the original purposes of IP law was to prevent the depletion of the commons by those with no incentives to contribute to it (Barnett, 2010; Coombe, 2003; McSherry, 2009). Before the Internet, fees, fines, and other sanctions were necessary to incentivize publishers to circulate academic work. Though digital technologies have obviated the need for many tangible expressions of knowledge, faculty members continue to use the traditional academic publishing system (structured around legally restrictive, subscription-based, print journals) because it is a direct route to professional incentives. Publishing in prestigious journals bolsters faculty reputations, and brings with it the standard rewards of tenure and promotion. Access to the scholarly work published in these journals—whether in print or in digital form—is most often closed, restricted by high subscription fees and pay walls. Faculty members who use these channels receive the reputational benefits associated with prestigious publications, but with limited visibility: closed access means that there are fewer people reading and responding to work, bypassing opportunities for its development. As Kleinman's chapter in this volume makes clear, the traditional system of scholarly publishing has evolved to become less effective at disseminating knowledge—the shared and fundamental mission of universities, publishers, and faculty members alike.

The Internet removes the print journal from the dissemination equation, effectively decentralizing research distribution, and allowing faculty researchers to circumvent legal and financial barriers by disseminating their research and coursework directly to their audience (Benkler & Nissenbaum, 2006). Citing openness norms and values of transparency, many academics have taken advantage of this newly discovered autonomy, prompting the development of a movement to open up scientific research to the public (Peter & Deimann, 2013).

The Openness Movement in Higher Education.   The academic commons is represented by the openness movement in higher education, which seeks to lift all unnecessary barriers to education and research for the good of society (Butcher, 2011; Peters & Britez, 2008). The word "openness" refers to transparency (Peters & Britez, 2008), and in its educational context, to the social desire for access to information. Openness is an idea and a collection of practices meant to increase access to higher education by the public.

The openness movement is often discussed in relation to the technological advancements that enabled its development (Peter & Deimann, 2013), but openness practices have a lengthy history in higher education, beginning with the correspondence courses of the 18th century (Casey, 2008; Matt & Fernandez, 2013). Courts have long recognized exceptions to IP laws based on commitments to openness in education. The fair use doctrine in U.S. Copyright law (17 U.S.C. §107, 1976) allows for the use of copyrighted material without permission or payment, when the benefit to society is greater than the damage to the copyright holder (AU Center for Social Media, 2009). Additionally, as Ahmadi's chapter in this volume explains, courts have recognized an academic exception to the "work made for hire" doctrine (1976) of the U.S. Copyright Act based on the unique aspects of the academic profession, including academic freedom and faculty autonomy (Porter, 2013).

Digital technologies have greatly facilitated access to information, permitting anyone with an Internet connection to consume and contribute to the pool of knowledge (Butcher & Hoosen, 2014). The openness movement is marked by a number of tech-based innovations in line with its mission to provide free access to knowledge for the public. Among them, open educational resources (OER), massive open online courses (MOOCs), and open access (OA) scholarly publishing are the most widely recognized. All or most of these innovations are made possible through open IP licenses, like those offered by Creative Commons (2013). These licenses expressly grant to users the freedom to use, reuse, and alter content to suit individual needs (Caswell, Henson, Jensen, & Wiley, 2008). Open licenses allow creators of educational works to retain some protection, but allow for access by the public free of charge. What these innovations have in common is that they are rooted in the idea of academic openness. To be clear, "openness" is merely an idea, but it is an idea around which a coalition has formed, and with the assistance of technology and the work of active, interested individuals, it is an idea around which institutional change can occur.

Though the openness movement has gained traction over the past 20 years, faculty who use and contribute to openness innovations represent a small minority of faculty members in the United States. This is because the politics of openness in education—addressed in the remainder of this chapter—are complex, involving various political, academic, and corporate players with very different interests and assumptions. The forces governing individual perceptions of the open/closed debate in the academy are subject to political and institutional processes resulting from competing narratives about the appropriate, ethical, and economical ways to govern common resources like knowledge.

Governing Knowledge.   The debate over IP law in education is essentially a governance question: What is the most effective, efficient, and socially beneficial way to govern a common pool of resources like knowledge? Or, as Boyle (2003) phrases it, to what extent should the commons be enclosed? Answers to this question differ, in part, based on the researcher's framework for understanding decision making and human behavior.

Along the spectrum of possible answers, three broadly defined "innovation regimes" can be used to govern common-pool resources (Barnett, 2010, p. 1764). These regimes are theoretical, but they are effective at demonstrating the wide range of risks and tradeoffs inherent in commons governance. They are the open-access, closed-access, and limited-access regimes, otherwise known as the "commons," "property," and "sharing" regimes (Barnett, p. 1764).

A commons regime is unregulated. It has no requirement that individuals contribute to the pool of knowledge and no limit on withdrawals (Barnett, 2010). Under a rational-choice framework, members of a commons regime have no incentives to contribute to the pool or refrain from removing knowledge from the pool. Beginning with Garett Hardin's infamous 1968 article in *Science*, the commons regime has come to be associated with its inescapably tragic outcome. The alleged "tragedy of the commons" (or the "free-rider" problem, Ostrom, 1990) is that absent state regulation, a rational man will deplete a common resource in pursuit of his own interest to the detriment of the collective good (Hardin, 1968).

On the opposite end of the spectrum is the property regime. The property regime is governed by laws, with strict requirements to contribute to the pool and limitations on withdrawal, under penalty of legal sanctions (Barnett, 2010). Proponents of the property regime argue that, in order to preserve the commons, it must be governed by an authoritative and coercive body, or a "leviathan" (Hardin, 1968, p. 314), in the form of privatization, laws, or government oversight. Opponents of the property regime argue that it is overregulated, and presents extensive barriers to innovation, consequences that are referred to as the "tragedy of the anticommons" (Heller & Eisenberg, 1998, p. 698).

The third form of governance is the sharing regime: halfway along the spectrum. It is more heavily regulated than the commons because the pool is governed by norms (as opposed to laws), which diminishes the risk of Hardin's (1968) tragic outcome. In the absence of formal laws, the sharing regime also avoids the high transaction costs associated with their enforcement, and thus places fewer constraints on innovation than a property regime.

Barnett (2010) argues that a true commons regime is an illusion because the cost of giving away a product or resource for free is always offset by some other funding source embedded within the economic structure of the organization. He argues that, contrary to popular belief, academic knowledge like scholarly research is not governed by a commons regime. It is neither regulated by formal laws nor is it completely unregulated. Rather, it functions by way of social norms of openness, which "mandate uncompensated forfeiture of private knowledge in exchange for the prospect of reputational prestige for innovation success" (Barnett, 2010, p. 1800). These norms are supported by norms of reciprocity that mandate giving attribution to prior innovators, and sanction harshly those who do not give credit. The university thus operates as an embedded sharing arrangement that is supported financially by a "coercive taxing authority (government) and/or voluntary philanthropic institutions" (Barnett, p. 1803). "Free research" (p. 1804) that is given away by faculty researchers (to publishers or to the public domain under an open access mandate) is not truly free at all, but bundled in one of three ways: It is linked to faculty teaching, and thus funded by tuition; it is sold to corporate partners through research contracts; or it is patented by universities who generate revenues for its use. Thus, the cost of labor required to produce the free resource is balanced by revenues from teaching, sales, or licensing.

Though useful to explain the spectrum of possibilities for commons governance, the three innovation regimes are merely models. A strict property regime would inevitably fail, as costly restrictions to access would preclude subsequent innovators from creating new knowledge, causing the pool to dry up. Similarly, a pure commons regime with no enforcement mechanisms is vulnerable to demise by a single self-interested individual intent on depleting the pool. Like the property regime, the commons regime is a heuristic, and either model, if institutionalized and taken to its extreme, can have unfortunate policy consequences.

Ways of Seeing the Property/Commons Debate

Following are two alternative perspectives on the debate over openness. The first is a critical discussion of the rational-choice perspective—a strictly economic paradigm underlying the dominant property regime, and founded on the assumption that rational individuals will always behave in accordance with their own self-interests. The second is the social constructivist perspective, which is based on the belief that individuals make meaning out of their worlds through experience and interaction with others. The purpose in presenting these two ways of seeing is to suggest that, though taken for granted, the dominant rational-choice perspective is not permanent, but based on a powerful narrative that has gained legitimacy in mainstream society. The property narrative is subject to institutional processes and may lose its legitimacy if challenged by a more compelling discourse, such as that espoused by the openness movement.

From a Rational-Choice Perspective.   Hardin's (1968) free-rider problem is based on the rational-choice theory of neoclassical economics— a theory for modeling individual behavior based on two overly broad assumptions: that people are all similarly motivated, and inherently selfish (Benkler, 2006). The framework has been used to shape policy for so long that the tragedy of the commons has come to be embedded in policy discourse as a sweeping cautionary tale to warn against communal governance and openness (Ostrom, 1990). Because private property rights are essential to the functioning of a capitalist society (Thurow, 2000), the commons and the very nature of collective governance are inconsistent with the dominant economic perspective in American society. As a result of the institutionalization of the free-rider problem, it is widely assumed that the property regime is the most effective form of governance for common-pool resources.

By contrast, Benkler (2006) argues that commons regimes can be more efficient than property regimes. For example, the open source software (OSS) movement resulted in products that are widely adopted and have surpassed those of the proprietary model in quality. Moreover, OSS continues to produce widespread, high-quality innovations without any form of centralized control. What is unique about Benkler's (2006) stance is that he departs from the rational-choice framework, taking a more optimistic approach to human behavior. He argues that commons-based peer production systems like Wikipedia and OSS evidence the capacity of individuals to cooperate, and that individuals with the same social interests are able to self-regulate and achieve a shared end absent markets or hierarchies. In contrast to opportunism and self-interest, motivations for participation in collective efforts include a sense of purpose, and the importance of contributing to the collective, public good (Benkler & Nissenbaum, 2006). Elinor Ostrom's (1990) Nobel Prize–winning study set out to empirically refute the tragedy of the commons discourse. Ostrom (1990) conducted lengthy studies of commons production systems from all over the world to determine if and how groups of interdependent individuals are able to organize and govern themselves to obtain sustainable, collective benefits in spite of temptations to act opportunistically. She found that commons can be successful with clearly defined boundaries, enforceable sanctions, mutual trust, and goals based on collective, as opposed to individual, outcomes. Ostrom (1990) argues that the "free-rider" problem, though not necessarily unfounded, is limited to situations with many independent actors who have limited communication and no mutual trust. She argues that Hardin's (1968) "tragedy" narrative is deeply intertwined with the rational-choice framework, which assumes a set of independent, self-interested actors. Ostrom's (1990) main argument is that the tragedy model is too frequently overgeneralized, and relied on too heavily to inform policy.

The ownership of knowledge is a social construction, but one so widely accepted that it seems a natural right of individuals that they would own their ideas (Fisk, 1998). Like the rational man of neoclassical economics, the tragedy of the commons is a heuristic, but one so deeply entrenched in economic and legal discourse that those who seek to challenge it are at an institutional disadvantage (Ostrom, 1990). From a rational-choice framework, collective governance is unrealistic, as is giving valuable knowledge away for free. However, the unregulated commons regime is equally oversimplified. OSS, Wikipedia, and Ostrom's (1990) communities are not true commons regimes because they are not entirely unregulated. Indeed, they rely on strictly enforced norms, clear boundaries, and common goals.

From a Social Constructivist Perspective.   From a social constructivist perspective, the property regime is just one possible narrative among many. Copyright, for example, is a legal and economic construction: a myth that has been shoehorned into a "mold of economic incentives" (Litman, 1991, p. 235). Viewed in this light, the purpose of IP law can be detached from its monetary value and understood, not as a reward for knowledge creation, but as a necessary mechanism to preserve the knowledge commons (Bollier, 2007).

Though deeply institutionalized in modern society (Fisk, 1998), IP has a long and fickle history. Boyle (2003) argues that there have been multiple IP revolutions that contributed to the construction of present-day IP law. The English "enclosure movement" was the process of fencing off common land and turning it into private property, lasting from the 15th to the 19th centuries (Boyle, 2003). The law is a reflection of changes in societal need. Individual conceptions of property are linked to the "structure of belief in the larger society, and in the legal system from which the property right came" (Boyle, 2003, p. 68). But law is also a highly political process, and often the result of strategic planning, intense advocacy, and carefully crafted stories.

> The goal of telling stories in law is not to entertain, or to terrify, or to illuminate life, as it usually is with storytelling outside the legal culture. The goal of storytelling in law is to persuade an official decisionmaker that one's story is true, to win the case, and thus to invoke the coercive force of the state on one's behalf. (Gewirtz, 1996)

Within the property discourse, the story of copyright begins with the myth of authorship (Litman, 1991). The dominant copyright narrative praises individualism, and copyright serves as a reward for individual talent and creativity. It assumes the presence of a single knowledge creator, while in reality, the production of a single work requires the labor of hundreds or thousands of individuals (Edelman, 1979). This is particularly true in academic research, where citation to the work of previous scholars is a prerequisite to publication.

Silbey (2010) argues that IP law is grounded in narrative theory. She frames the "access movements" as presenting a counter narrative to the property regime, and argues that the dominance of the latter is due to widespread acceptance of a compelling origin story. The property discourse is based on a story that "glorifies and valorizes enchanted moments of individual creation, discovery or identity in order to justify exclusivity and monopoly" (Silbey, 2010, p. 200), and it secures its own institutional power by treating alternative interpretations as piracy and appropriation (McSherry, 2009).

The property discourse asserts that restrictions to knowledge and innovation are necessary to promote social progress, and so opening up educational materials to the public exhausts the knowledge pool. By contrast, the discourse of the openness movement suggests that putting a price tag on knowledge precludes access, contrary to the interests of the public good, and is thus inherently unethical. These polarized stories may be effective in a debate, but as discussed earlier, the reality of each opposing stance is far more complex than a story of heroes and villains (Ruebottom, 2013). Rather, the valence, or emotional quality, attached to narratives of property and openness are socially constructed and often politically motivated. The dominance of the property regime over the commons can be explained, in part, as the result of its proponents' ability to tell a more compelling and enduring story that is consistent with the audience's understanding of their social world.

Implications for Faculty and the Academic Profession

In recent years, there has been evidence of an institutional shift in perceptions about academic openness, prompted by a growing awareness of the futility of middlemen disseminators of knowledge, like for-profit publishers. The dissemination of academic work has long been the province of market-driven organizations. Such an arrangement is effective so long as competition drives productivity. However, the corporate monopolization of academic research has obscured one major purpose for which higher education and publishers exist, which is to communicate that research to the public. Faculty members, independent researchers, and openness advocates have assembled to fight for open access, with increasingly positive responses from governments and other funders of education. If openness practices are to endure, then institutions must evolve to fit the current technological, social, and economic climate in which the academy is situated.

The tenure structure is one such institution that perpetuates the property regime by incentivizing faculty to disseminate their work through traditional (and restrictive) channels, such as prestigious peer-reviewed journals that are owned by large corporate publishers. Though many leading universities, including Harvard, MIT, and the University of California system, have instituted open access policies, these policies require only that faculty post their already published works into open access repositories. Though these policies promote openness on their face, they do little to alter perceptions about open access methods of dissemination. Incentives for tenure and promotion remain largely unchanged, and offer little to no support for faculty to publish in or develop open access journals. Balance requires a move toward greater openness in research, along with policies that incentivize faculty to use open forums instead of the same top tier journals in the field.

Changing the scholarly communication system is particularly difficult because the whole of scholarship covering the last century is "owned" by many different institutional participants—publishers own scholarly articles, while universities often lay claim to faculty inventions and digital courseware (see Rhoades chapter) (American Association of University Professors, 2013; Loggie et al., 2008; Lape, 1992; Lynch, 2008; Packard, 2001). However, the responsibilities of these participants, at their most basic levels, are the same—to disseminate knowledge in pursuit of social progress (Lynch, 2008). It is discovering where the paths of stakeholders diverge that is essential to creating lasting institutional change.

Balancing ownership rights cannot be done through a single voice or piece of legislation. It is an ongoing struggle to ensure that the rights of faculty members, universities, and publishers be fairly represented in policymaking efforts, but it is unlikely that this will happen until each group recognizes its common duty, and finds an effective middle ground between the property and commons regimes. Though good storytelling may be a valuable political strategy, within the complex and loosely coupled academy (Birnbaum, 1988), compromise and collaboration may be more efficient in achieving a common mission.

Conclusion

This chapter introduced the concept of academic openness as the antithesis to IP. The purpose of the chapter was both to educate faculty about the broader legal and philosophical environment surrounding IP in higher education, and to propose a path to institutional change through openness advocacy. Though the politics of openness in education are complex, they are often articulated by both sides of the political debate as extreme opposing narratives. The openness movement in higher education seeks to restore balance between the open and closed narratives by raising awareness among faculty and researchers about alternatives to the restrictive law-based systems of dissemination. Universities and funders have responded positively to the open access mission in recent years, but institutional change requires more than a single voice or mandate. It requires, among other things, an overhaul of the traditional incentive structure, including greater institutional support for open access by universities through financial assistance and professional incentives for faculty to publish in open access journals. Change requires that stakeholders in higher education—faculty, universities, and publishers—recognize their shared responsibility to the public to disseminate knowledge in pursuit of social progress.

References

American Association of University Professors. (2013). *Education action and toolkit* [Web page]. Retrieved from http://www.aaup.org/get-involved/issue-campaigns/intellectual-property-risk

AU Center for Social Media. (2009). *Code of best practices in fair use for OpenCourseWare*.

Barnett, J. M. (2010). The illusion of the commons. *Berkeley Technology Law Journal, 25*, 1751.

Benkler, Y. (2006) *The wealth of networks: How social production transforms markets and freedom.* New Haven, CT: Yale University Press.

Benkler, Y., & Nissenbaum, H. (2006). Commons-based peer production and virtue. *The Journal of Political Philosophy, 14*(4), 394–419.

Birnbaum, R. (1988). *How Colleges Work: The cybernetics of academic organization and leadership.* San Francisco: Jossey-Bass.

Bollier, D. (2007). The growth of the commons paradigm. In C. Hess & E. Ostrom (Eds.), *Understanding knowledge as a commons: From theory to practice* (pp. 27–40). Cambridge, MA: MIT Press.

Boyle, J. (2003). The second enclosure movement and the construction of the public domain. *Law and Contemporary Problems,* 33–74.

Boyle, J. (2008). *The public domain: Enclosing the commons of the mind.* New Haven, CT: Yale University Press.

Butcher, N. (2011). *A basic guide to open educational resources.* Commonwealth of Learning & UNESCO.

Butcher, N., & Hoosen, S. (2014). *How openness impacts on higher education,* IITE Policy Brief. Moscow: UNESCO, Institute for Information Technologies in Education, pp. 12.

Casey, D. M. (2008). The historical development of distance education through technology. *TechTrends, 52*(2), 45.

Caswell, T., Henson, S., Jensen, M., & Wiley, D. (2008). Open content and open educational resources: Enabling universal education. *The International Review of Research in Open and Distance Learning, 9*(1).

Coombe, R. (2003). Fear, hope, and longing for the future of authorship and a revitalized public domain in global regimes of intellectual property. *DePaul Law Review, 52,* 1171–1191.

Creative Commons. (2013). General format. Retrieved June 26, 2015, from http://creativecommons.org/about

Edelman, B. (1979). *Ownership of the image: Elements for a Marxist theory of law.* London, UK: Routledge.

Fisk, C. (1998). Removing the "Fuel of Interest" from the "Fire of Genius": Law and the employee-inventor, 1830–1930. *University of Chicago Law Review.*

Gewirtz, P. (1996). Narrative and rhetoric in the law. In P. Brooks & P. Gewirtz (Eds.), *Law's stories: Narrative and rhetoric in the law* (pp. 2–12). New Haven, CT: Yale University Press.

Gumport, P. J., & Sporn, B. (1999). *Institutional adaptation: Demands for management reform and university administration.* Palo Alto, CA: National Center for Postsecondary Improvement Stanford University School of Education.

Hardin, G. (1968). The tragedy of the commons. *Science, 162*(3859), 1243–1248.

Heller, M., & Eisenberg, R. (1998). Can patents deter innovation? The anticommons in biomedical research. *Science, 280*(5364), 698–701.

Hervieux, C., Gedajlovic, E., & Turcotte, M. F. B. (2010). The legitimization of social entrepreneurship. *Journal of Enterprising Communities: People and Places in the Global Economy, 4*(1), 37–67.

Loggie, K. A., Barron, A. E., Gulitz, E., Hohlfeld, T. N., Kromrey, J. D., & Sweeney, P. (2008). Intellectual property and online courses. *Quarterly Review of Distance Education: Volume 8 Book, 109.*

Lape, L. G. (1992). Ownership of copyrightable works of university professors: The interplay between the copyright act and university copyright policies. *Villanova Law Review, 37,* 22–269.

Litman, J. (1991). Copyright as myth. *University of Pittsburgh Law Review, 53,* 235.

Lynch, C. A. (2008). A matter of mission: Information technology and the future of higher education. *The Tower and the Cloud: Higher Education in the Age of Cloud Computing,* 43–50.

Matt, S., & Fernandez, L. (2013). Before MOOCs, "Colleges of the Air." *The Chronicle of Higher Education.*

McSherry, C. (2009). *Who owns academic work? Battling for control of intellectual property.* Cambridge, MA: Harvard University Press.

Ostrom, E. (1990). *Governing the commons: The evolution of institutions for collective action.* New York, NY: Cambridge University Press.

Packard, A. (2001). Copyright or copy wrong: An analysis of university claims to faculty work. *Communication and Law Policy, 7,* 275–316.

Peter, S., & Deimann, M. (2013, January–March). On the role of openness in education: A historical reconstruction. *Open Praxis, 5*(1), 7–14.

Peters, M. (2003). Classical political economy and the role of universities in the New Knowledge Economy [1], *Globalisation, Societies and Education, 1*(2).

Peters, M., & Britez, R. (2008). Open Education and Education for Openness. *Educational futures: Rethinking theory and practice. 27.*

Porter, J. (2013). MOOCs, "Courses," and the question of faculty and student copyrights. *The CCCC-IP annual: Top intellectual property developments of 2012.* pp. 2–18. Intellectual property caucus of the Conference on College Composition and Communication.

Ruebottom, T. (2013). The microstructures of rhetorical strategy in social entrepreneurship: Building legitimacy through heroes and villains. *Journal of Business Venturing, 28*(1), 98–116.

Silbey, J. (2010). Comparative tales of origins and access: Intellectual property and the rhetoric of social change, 16:1. *Case Western Reserve Law Review, 195.*

Stiglitz, J. (1999). Knowledge as a global public good. In I. Kaul, I. Grunberg, & M. Stern (Eds.), *Global public goods* (pp. 308–325). New York, NY: Oxford University Press.

Thurow, L. C. (2000). Globalization: The product of a knowledge-based economy. *Annals of the American Academy of Political and Social Science, 570,* 19–31.

U.S. Copyright Act. (1976). 17 U.S.C. §107.

SAMANTHA BERNSTEIN-SIERRA *is an attorney and PhD candidate of urban education policy at the University of Southern California's Rossier School of Education. Her research centers on public/private tensions in higher education, organizational theory, openness in higher education research and teaching, and the future of the academic profession.*

5

This chapter analyzes collective bargaining agreements in 4-year institutions of higher education, examining language surrounding ownership, use, and distribution of the proceeds of intellectual property in distance education, and identifying ways in which the public good can be, and occasionally is, built in to contractual provisions.

Negotiating Whose Property It Is, for the Public Good

Gary Rhoades

How are the ownership, use, and distribution of proceeds from the intellectual property in distance education that is created by faculty members negotiated in collective bargaining agreements (CBAs), and how can the public good be embedded in contractual provisions? Those two questions frame this chapter. In order to address those questions, I analyze 149 contracts in 4-year colleges and universities. My answers to the two framing questions speak to what is found in the contracts and what could be negotiated in intellectual property provisions about distance education. The findings point to how negotiations are playing out in whose property distance education is, and to how these negotiations could more fully play out in serving the public good.

The Broader Context of Bargaining

The contracts being analyzed have been negotiated in a broader social context. That context includes an increasingly predominant academic capitalism, heightened emphasis on distance education, and an ongoing negotiation between academic labor and management over the academy's direction. The past several decades have witnessed the ascendance of an "academic capitalist knowledge/learning regime" (Slaughter & Leslie, 1997; Slaughter & Rhoades, 2004). That involves universities' aggressive pursuit of new revenue streams, capitalizing on existing activities and relationships or developing new circuits of knowledge production to transform the knowledge into a commodity to be sold on the open market. Patenting dramatizes this, with universities developing new interstitial offices and

New Directions for Higher Education, no. 177, Spring 2017 © 2017 Wiley Periodicals, Inc.
Published online in Wiley Online Library (wileyonlinelibrary.com) • DOI: 10.1002/he.20226

managerial capacity to transfer knowledge to the private sector. Such activity is contingent on renegotiating state, federal, and institutional policies and on establishing new, more tightly concentrated relations with the private sector and with intermediating organizations that shape the direction of research (Slaughter, Thomas, Johnson, & Barringer, 2014).

Although it is not recognized by many scholars or discussed by policy makers, so, too, do new circuits of production in instruction, as with distance education, involve a renegotiation surrounding property rights. New structures emerge within universities to manage and market this commodity as do new relations with private and intermediating organizations that expand markets for distance education products. University policies, as well as state and federal policies about distance education, copyright, intellectual property ownership, (re)use, and profits are being (re)negotiated.

Distance Education and Intellectual Property Rights

Much has been written about the growth of distance education in American higher education. Little has been written about the intellectual property rights involved, and about the implications that negotiating these rights has for higher education's public purposes. Much of the policy interest in and discourse about distance education relates to its potential and claim as a delivery model that reduces cost and increases access and quality (Breneman, Pusser, & Turner, 2006; Noble, 2001). Little work empirically considers how high-tech innovations that monetize higher education and privatize knowledge are negotiating these property interests and how these implicate universities' role in creating quality, accessible knowledge for the public domain. That will center this chapter's analysis of CBAs—how labor and management are negotiating ownership of distance education materials, who has control of (re)use, and claims on the proceeds, as well as the extent to which that negotiation can and could speak to the public good.

Intellectual property generally, and distance education models in particular are generally framed as innovation, with innovation being seen as contributing to the public good. The prevailing belief, contested by the open source movement, is that innovation, which contributes to public benefit, must be incentivized with private benefit for the inventor—that is at the core of the policy regime of academic capitalism. Although not generally acknowledged, the same calculus holds in distance education, which involves negotiating private ownership of the intellectual property involved, which is believed also to serve the public good. The potential public benefits of this innovation are quite clear in that distance education is said to increase access and quality while reducing cost. The contract provisions surrounding distance education property rights offer insight into the extent to which such public interest concerns are being addressed in negotiations.

NEW DIRECTIONS FOR HIGHER EDUCATION • DOI: 10.1002/he

The Conceptual Foundations of the Study

The collective negotiation of professional autonomy and managerial discretion in collective bargaining has received little scholarly attention. Historically, the little literature that exists has generally been framed from a managerial perspective, asking how unionizing will affect "collegial" aspects of academia (Rhoades, 1998). The perspective is more an internal consideration of the academic effects of unionization than a concern for how the negotiation impacts the public good (Ladd & Lipset, 1973). More recently, some scholarship has concentrated on quality issues surrounding the working conditions of faculty in "contingent" positions off the tenure track. Scholars have studied "best practices" for quality education in unionized and nonunionized settings (Baldwin & Chronister, 2001; Kezar & Sam, 2013). In this chapter, I take a next step, focusing on the extent to which and how the public good is built into contractual language on intellectual property rights in distance education. My interest is in how collective bargaining can expand the public domain in higher education.

The Data and the Focus

The data analyzed in this chapter come from a national database of CBAs in higher education called Higher Education Contract Analysis System (HECAS). Produced and maintained by the National Education Association, it includes 494 CBAs covering college and university faculty, including 149 in 4-year institutions and systems (most public colleges and universities are parts of systems, and contracts generally cover multiple institutions in the system—so the contracts cover a far larger number of institutions than 149). The contracts include those negotiated by affiliates of all three major faculty unions as well as of independent unions, and constitute 81% of all CBAs covering faculty in 4-year institutions found in a national directory (Moriarty & Savarese, 2012).

For the purposes of this chapter, the empirical focus is on intellectual property provisions surrounding distance education. Given space limitations, the chapter does not address intellectual property provisions surrounding other technology-mediated instruction (e.g., hybrid classes) or other forms of intellectual property, such as patents. Nor does it address clauses related to academic governance in developing and approving distance education courses, though these affect quality control, and thus the public good.

Analytically, the chapter focuses on two fulcrums that shape property ownership, use, and distribution of profits: (1) To what extent do agreements reflect a balance between professors' autonomous control of the curricular materials they create and teach, and managers' discretion over and the institution's ownership and control of employees' work?; (2) To what extent does contractual language invoke the public interest, whether indirectly (as in a focus on quality), or in direct references to the public welfare?

The data have some clear limitations. First, there are far more public than there are private universities with CBAs, although there are definite parallels in the form of the CBA provisions and the intellectual property provisions of elite private and public research universities (see Slaughter & Rhoades, 2004). Second, although higher education has relatively high union density, CBAs nationally still cover only a little more than one-quarter (28%) of faculty nationally, and there is an underrepresentation of elite research universities in these numbers. Third, I focus only on 4-year institutions, although much distance education is done in community colleges. And fourth, although the CBAs can tell us a lot about the formal terms and conditions of employment, there may be informal and other ways outside the contract that faculty and the institution intersect with and address the public good. Nevertheless, there is considerable value in identifying what is being formally negotiated in a significant portion of American higher education by way of intellectual property rights in distance education, what is being largely left out, and what possibilities there are for more fully incorporating matters of the public good into the CBAs.

Ownership provisions, which also deal with (re)use and the distribution of profits are the most common clauses (33 contracts) regarding distance education in the CBAs of 4-year institutions. The findings are organized around those three issues. What determines ownership, and what are the patterns, if any in who owns the intellectual property produced by faculty in distance education? What conditions surround the use and reuse of distance education course materials. And what patterns if any characterize the distribution of proceeds from distance education?

Ownership of Intellectual Property.   Three points are striking in determining ownership. A key factor is whether "substantial university resources" have been used in creating the property. Moreover, some contracts define the creation of materials as a "work for hire" if the faculty member is paid for developing those materials. Finally, only a few contracts refer to forms of public subsidy and the public good beyond the employing institution (see below the example from Ferris State University).

In most cases, the determining factor regarding ownership is whether the creation of the property involves "substantial use of university resources" (no such language is found in relation to the creation of nondistance education courses). Generally, if it does not (and sometimes even if it does), then the faculty member owns the property. Indeed, in unionized settings with language that speaks to intellectual property (a minority of the contracts), the contracts tend to accord ownership to the faculty creator, more so than is the case in nonunionized settings (see Slaughter & Rhoades, 2004).

The particular language can vary (e.g., some contracts refer to "extraordinary use"). But the key is wording that suggests greater than normal use of resources. Some contracts define this in some detail, and in ways that benefit faculty ownership (though overall, most contracts do not accord ownership to faculty).

> [I]t is understood that online and other modes of distance course delivery and development generally do not constitute the substantial use of University resources, and that instructional materials developed by a faculty member in the process of delivering the course shall be the property of the faculty member. (University of Nebraska, Kearney)

> C. University-Supported Work. If the University provides assistance (hereinafter labeled "extra-ordinary assistance") beyond that usually accorded to faculty, other employees, or students in their work, then the University may claim ownership of the copyright to works produced, unless the creator obtains written authorization from the University before using those resources. In general, a faculty member's obligation to produce scholarly works does not constitute a specific University assignment for purposes of the "work for hire" doctrine. Unless specifically identified as extra-ordinary assistance and agreed to by the faculty in writing before receipt of such assistance, the following do not constitute extra-ordinary assistance: (i) payment of a regular salary; (ii) summer research grants; (iii) professional leave; (iv) release time resulting from reduced instructional assignments as provided for by contract or University policy; (v) the personal use of office and library facilities; (vi) the use of personal computers, or reasonable data and word processing services. Extra-ordinary assistance includes, but is not limited to, financial assistance, extra technical help such as assistance from University computer programmers or technicians, or greater than normal use of such University facilities that an outside user would be charged for use. (Cleveland State University)

The reference in the Cleveland State language to the "work for hire" doctrine leads to a second consideration in determining ownership. Was a faculty member tasked with that assignment, and paid for it accordingly, such that the university has claim on the ownership of the property that was created? In some cases, the answer is yes.

> Courses developed at the request of the college as defined by the purchase agreement and for which the faculty member receives additional compensation are considered a work for hire and the property of the college. (Nebraska State University)

Beyond the brief reference above in the Cleveland State University language, the contract has a clause specifically delimiting what does and does not constitute work for hire.

NEW DIRECTIONS FOR HIGHER EDUCATION • DOI: 10.1002/he

A. Works for Hire. Copyrightable materials produced by University faculty as the result of direct work assignments to meet specific objectives or as an assigned University duty other than general academic research and normal teaching assignments are "works for hire" for which copyrights belong to the University. A faculty member's general obligation to produce scholarly works does not constitute a specific University assignment for purposes of the "work for hire" doctrine, nor do research grants for specific scholarly projects provided by the University to faculty members fall under the "work for hire" doctrine. Unless the subject of a written agreement as described in Section 27.13.C., modification of an existing University course to incorporate "hybrid" eLearning components or for delivery via distance education modalities does not, in and of itself, constitute a specific University assignment for purposes of the "work for hire" doctrine. (Cleveland State University)

It is striking that apart from the "use of university resources," other forms of public subsidy, which are substantial, and other considerations of the public interest, are left out of the vast majority of contractual provisions on distance education. Consider the infrastructure that supports distance education that was created and/or is sustained by public investment. The Internet's creation was publicly funded. The employment of the faculty member, and that faculty member's ability and legitimacy to distribute a course inheres not in a private "firm," but in a public college or university. Students' ability to access and pay for distance education courses are facilitated by a range of public policies and sources and sites of public infrastructure, as well as by public financial aid (indeed, this has become a huge issue in regard to proprietary higher education). Essentially, distance education is underwritten by various levels and types of public, governmental support and investment. But the policies leave the broader public with no claim, nor do they address how the public welfare can be served by distance education. Innovation is assumed to be good, and to require incentivization for the faculty member and/or institution.

One exception points to the possibility for referencing the public interest.

A. Introduction.

Ferris State University is dedicated to teaching, scholarly activity, and the extension of knowledge and services to the public, particularly the citizens of Michigan. The University community recognizes its responsibility to produce and disseminate knowledge. Inherent within this responsibility is the need to encourage the production of creative and scholarly works and the development of new and useful materials, devices, processes, and other Intellectual Property, some of which may have potential commercial value. These activities contribute to the professional development of the individuals involved, enhance the reputation of the University in which they work, provide additional educational opportunities for students, and promote the public welfare.

NEW DIRECTIONS FOR HIGHER EDUCATION • DOI: 10.1002/he

Such language in the preamble of an article is nonbinding in terms of specific practices but symbolically significant in foregrounding the university's public purposes, no matter who owns the property. Such explicit references in contracts feature the public functions of higher education institutions amid the negotiation of private property interests.

One could imagine as well as taking a next step with such language in featuring the importance of keeping publicly subsidized intellectual property in the public domain. The clearest example is the open access movement and the concept of creative commons, which are entirely lacking in the contracts (see also Molly Kleinman's chapter in this volume). Further, there are ways of ensuring that intellectual property, even when commercialized, retains some aspects of open access in the public domain. The most obvious example is faculty's scholarly publications. Those are generally copyrighted by publishing houses with which the author signs an agreement. Those are generally copyrighted by publishing houses that in the case of books the faculty signs a contract with. At the same time, these publications are put in the public domain, in libraries.

(Re) Use of Distance Education Course(s)/Materials.   Ownership of intellectual property is one matter. The use and reuse of that property is quite another. Consider the following scenario in the case of distance education: A faculty member may create a course and teach it the first time it is offered, but can others be assigned the course in subsequent semesters? Can the institution assign the course to a third party outside the institution, whether a faculty member outside the bargaining unit, another college, or a for-profit provider? Can the course be delivered in perpetuity without revision? Each of these questions bears on quality and the public interest.

Several contracts situate the use and reuse of distance education materials in the faculty member/creator. Some speak to creators' first rights to reteach the course and control over their use of it, as in two clauses from the University of Nebraska, Kearney:

> The Unit Member(s) who originally created the distance education course retains the right to use his or her course as he or she deems appropriate ...

> (i) The decision to rebroadcast a course rests with the instructor, Department Chair, and the Dean of the College; however, the administration shall have the final prerogative regarding rebroadcast consistent with (ii) and (iii) below.

> (ii) If an entire previously-recorded course is offered for credit in a subsequent semester, the Unit Member(s) who created and/or taught the course shall be notified and given first consideration to administer the re-broadcast of the course. If the Unit Member(s) who created the course declines to administer the re-broadcast the sponsoring Department may assign another Unit Member to teach the course. The course will be taught either in-load or as an overload. (iii) If a decision is made to revise the course, the Unit Member(s)

who created the course shall have the first right to revise the course. If the Unit Member(s) decline, the Department may offer the course to another Unit Member(s) for revision.

A few contracts are even stronger by way of ensuring professional autonomy. A particularly strong example in this regard is the contract of Western Michigan University.

30.§5 Courses and course delivery shall not be recorded (audio- or videotaped or digitally captured) without prior knowledge and consent of the faculty member. Such recordings are not to be re-used without the written consent of the faculty member. ... 30.§5.1 The faculty member (or an appropriate faculty body) who creates the course content materials (or adapts a pre-existing course to an eLearning format) for use in eLearning shall exercise control over the future use, modification, and distribution of instructional material, and shall determine whether the material should be revised or withdrawn from use.

This language affords the faculty creator absolute control of the property. And it does so in considerable part in the name of quality control. Such quality control ensures that a course does not continue to be offered without being updated. The more common reuse language simply gives the creator of the course first choice in teaching it.

The contract language of Rider University is also strong and declarative, but it takes another approach to the matter of use.

Any recording of a Distance Learning course will occur only with the permission of the instructor and will remain the property of the instructor. Neither the instructor nor the University shall sell the recording to a third party for use outside the University's academic curriculum. (Rider University)

The Rider contract prevents commodification of the property by commercializing it in other institutions. The intellectual creations of the faculty are kept in the public domain.

Overwhelmingly, the contracts address intellectual property issues in distance education simply in terms of the individual course and faculty member. What is largely overlooked is the public interest implications of the overall modality of distance delivery. Many claims have been made regarding distance education increasing access, reducing cost, and increasing quality. It would make sense, then, to assess in an ongoing way the extent to which distance education is educationally (and cost) effective. It would also make sense to assess the extent to which it is working for particular student populations.

One example of such contract language points to the possibility and desirability of negotiating intellectual property rights with an eye to the larger public benefit. It is significant that this exception is Chicago State University, an institution with an urban, lower income student population that is disproportionately students of color.

> (3) Each academic department and/or division in conjunction with the Distance Education Committee shall (a) develop, monitor and review distance education offerings and make recommendations for change and improvement; (b) provide the methodology to evaluate the effectiveness of the distance learning offerings;

> (c) develop a procedure that ensures adequate advisement for students registering for online courses. ... f. The Office of Distance Learning shall (1) be consulted concerning pre-packaged web-based materials or courses and monitor and evaluate the effectiveness of the online service provider, its delivery of services, and compliance with the terms and conditions of the contract and ensure that the contract meets University and student needs; ... (3) provide technical support and customer service to faculty teaching a distance education course and to students taking a distance education course; ... (5) assist in the assessment of student capability to use education technology.

There is value in evaluating the educational effectiveness of distance education for particular populations of students—for instance, the growth populations of lower income, students of color. Such students may not fit the prevailing image of technologically well-equipped and proficient students; many, for instance, do not have high-speed Internet access at home. The public good is served by attending to the value of innovations that support those student populations who are the growing majority of students in K–12 education nationally. At present, the clauses overwhelmingly are focused on capitalizing on the expansion of distance education, in faculty and institutions laying claim to the proceeds, with almost no attention to factoring in the public mission of higher education.

Distribution of Proceeds From Distance Education.   Separate from the issue of ownership is also the matter of distributing the proceeds from the sale of intellectual property. Even if the institution owns the property, the faculty creator of the distance education materials may still receive a portion of the "profits," and vice versa. The rationale underlying most of the language here is the need for a financial return on investment. There is the university's investment in the faculty member and in the creation of the intellectual property (in the use of institutional resources). And there is the professor's investment of professional expertise and time in developing the course.

One example of such language captures an overriding pattern in the contracts, that the "investors" in creating property are largely seen as the institution and the inventor.

NEW DIRECTIONS FOR HIGHER EDUCATION • DOI: 10.1002/he

The Employer, however, may not sell or re-transmit in future semesters any such recording except under the terms of a written Agreement between the Employer and the Faculty Member providing each party with a fifty percent (50%) interest in the net profits from either the sale or rebroadcast. (The University of Hawaii)

Virtually all of the contractual provisions on distance education intellectual property speak to the proceeds in terms of the two parties at the bargaining table, management and labor, with labor being the individual faculty member, not the faculty as a whole.

Such a construction of claimants seems to make sense. Both institutions and individual faculty members are central players in creating intellectual property. But one could imagine rewarding a broader set of claimants within the institution. And indeed, much intellectual property language on patenting does that, recognizing the role of labs, departments, and even colleges in the creation of intellectual property, and identifying these entities as recipients at least of minor shares of the proceeds (Slaughter & Rhoades, 2004). Similar claimants could also be rewarded in distance education, as there are sometimes departmental, lab, and college roles in creating materials, and as other professionals and graduate students may be involved in developing courses.

One could imagine a broader set of claimants beyond the institution as well. One contract (Saginaw Valley State University) provides an example.

In the event a faculty member develops or prepares materials which are required to be purchased by students in a class taught at SVSU, no part of the revenue for that sale shall be retained as the personal income of that faculty member. If such a sale to students yields a royalty or other payment to the faculty member he/she shall remit the entire amount to the SVSU Foundation. All such revenue will be deposited into one of the SVSU Faculty Association Scholarship Funds as designated by the faculty member.

A first nod to the public interest is the provision that when materials developed by the faculty member are used in a course and students at the university are charged a fee for taking the course, neither the faculty creator nor the institution can pocket the proceeds. A second is that the proceeds from charges to students at the university are put into its foundation, in a fund for scholarships.

Summary

In a time of growing academic capitalism universities are increasingly laying claim to the creative products of faculty work as a new revenue stream. That tendency is heightened in public universities in the face of patterns in state appropriations. Similarly, amid stagnant salaries and declining benefits, faculty have increasingly come to regard distance education courses as another source of income (from royalties and from the ability with this delivery mode to teach higher levels of and sometimes higher paid overload and summer teaching). Thus, the first major finding of this chapter is not surprising—there are few intellectual property provisions about distance education that address the public good. Both parties to the negotiation have articulated and amplified a focus on distance education intellectual property as revenue generation, narrowing the public domain.

A second major finding in analyzing provisions in the 149 CBAs of 4-year colleges and universities is that a vast majority of contracts do not have such language. Less than a quarter (22%) even have provisions addressing intellectual property in distance education. Not defining such matters relegates the disposition of ownership, (re)use, and proceeds to the realm of management rights. In short, there is extensive managerial discretion in distance education property rights.

A third finding is that, of those contracts that do address intellectual property rights in distance education, most recognize faculty as owners of the property if there is not substantial use of university resources, while others define such use narrowly and in some cases according ownership to faculty even if use is substantial. Moreover, many accord faculty creators first claim in the use and reuse of materials they create, and in having a share of the proceeds of the property they create even if substantial university resources have been utilized in creating the course. Some accord faculty the right to determine whether and how distance education materials they have created will be used.

Notwithstanding the overriding patterns, there are examples in the contracts of ways in which the public interest can be incorporated into intellectual property language. This is not just a matter of choosing between or balancing "profits" from intellectual property and an open access approach. One mechanism is to embed mention of the public welfare into contract language in any of several ways. Preambles or introductions of clauses could embed language about the public good purposes and values at play in creating intellectual property in distance education. Moreover, in clauses about use and reuse of distance education property, there are examples of contractual language that speak to the public welfare in three ways: (1) assessing the educational effectiveness and cost efficiency of this modality for students generally and for the growing and historically underserved demographics of students in particular; (2) assuring that students are trained and supported in the use of distance education materials, toward the end of reducing the digital divide and the ongoing achievement gap; and (3) ensuring that materials are revised and updated and provided to a high-quality standard. Finally, in clauses about the distribution of proceeds from distance education, there are examples of how to expand the range of beneficiaries to balance private interests with the broader public interest.

NEW DIRECTIONS FOR HIGHER EDUCATION • DOI: 10.1002/he

One other creative example stems from considering the roughly half of the faculty members nationally who are employed in part-time positions. Although many of the 149 contracts analyzed for this chapter covered some categories of part-time faculty, the growth in adjunct organizing is in stand-alone units, often in 4-year institutions—one notable example is George Washington University, the first success in a series of "metro" campaign drives nationally (Rhoades, 2013). Ironically, despite the limited investment of universities in such faculty, and these professors' lack of access often to even the most routine instructional resources, adjunct only units have not negotiated distance education property rights even though these faculty often teach such technology-mediated courses.

For the above reasons, it has been suggested elsewhere (Rhoades, 2013) that adjunct faculty within metropolitan areas should create curricular cooperatives in the public interest. The current push is to monetize distance education in ways that tap into massive, global markets, and that in turn are based in mass-produced and mass-marketed intellectual property that is all too distant from the realities of most students, particularly of those in the growth demographics that have historically not been well served by higher education. What if adjunct faculty, who are tied to and embedded in metropolitan (and rural) regions were to develop locally relevant curricula more closely attuned to the lives of their students locally? And what if that intellectual property was grounded in and owned by regional associations and unions of faculty? That might lead to new ways of creatively conceiving and pursuing the public welfare and interests of specific locales.

In sum, at present, intellectual property rights in distance education are largely being negotiated as if the two parties at the table, labor and management, are the only interested parties, or are the only parties implicated by the negotiations. Yet that is not the case. Creating intellectual property, including in distance education, has always featured the value of its contribution to the public welfare. Even amid the ascendance of academic capitalism, and the dominance of its pervasive logic that the public benefits from private gain, collective bargaining offers feasible strategies for recentering the higher education's public purposes. As I wrote over a decade ago, "I am not suggesting that we take vows of poverty and sequester ourselves like medieval monks and nuns. But there are reasonable alternatives to the privatization of academic knowledge" (Rhoades, 2001, p. 43). Contract provisions offer examples of alternatives that protect and even expand the public domain in negotiating intellectual property in distance education.

References

Baldwin, R. G., & Chronister, J. I. (2001). *Teaching without tenure: Policies and practices for a new era*. Baltimore, MD: The Johns Hopkins University Press.
Breneman, D. W., Pusser, B., & Turner, S. E. (2006). *Earning for learning: The rise of for-profit universities*. Albany: State University of New York Press.

Kezar, A., & Sam, C. (2013). Institutionalizing equitable policies and practices for contingent faculty. *The Journal of Higher Education, 84*(1), 56–87.

Ladd, E. C. Jr., & Lipset, S. M. (1973). *Professors, unions, and American higher education.* New York, NY: McGraw-Hill.

Moriarty, J., & Savarese, M. (2012). *Directory of faculty contracts and bargaining agents in institutions of higher education.* New York, NY: National Center for the Study of Collective Bargaining in Higher Education and the Professions.

Noble, D. F. (2001). *Digital diploma mills: The automation of higher education.* New York, NY: Monthly Review Press.

Rhoades, G. (1998). *Managed professionals: Unionized faculty and restructuring academic labor.* Albany: State University of New York Press.

Rhoades, G. (2001). Whose property is it?: Negotiating with the university. *Academe, 87*(5), 38–43.

Rhoades, G. (2013, Fall). Disruptive innovations for adjunct faculty: Common sense for the common good. *Thought & Action, 29,* 71–86.

Slaughter, S., & Leslie, L. (1997). *Academic capitalism. Politics, policies, and the entrepreneurial university.* Baltimore, MD: The Johns Hopkins University Press.

Slaughter, S., & Rhoades, G. (2004). *Academic capitalism and the new economy: Markets, state, and higher education.* Baltimore, MD: The Johns Hopkins University Press.

Slaughter, S., Thomas, S. L., Johnson, D., & Barringer, S. N. (2014). Institutional conflict of interest: The role of interlocking directorates in the scientific relationships between universities and the corporate sector. *The Journal of Higher Education, 85*(1), 1–25.

GARY RHOADES *is professor and director of the Center for the Study of Higher Education at the University of Arizona's College of Education. From 2009 through 2011, he served as general secretary of the American Association of University Professors in Washington, DC.*

NEW DIRECTIONS FOR HIGHER EDUCATION • DOI: 10.1002/he

This chapter describes the protectionist and access functions of intellectual property for the teaching and research work of university faculty. The degree to which an individual piece of IP is protected or made accessible to others depends in large measure on its market-related characteristics, including costs of production, availability of substitutes, and repurposing potential.

University Faculty and the Value of Their Intellectual Property: Comparing IP in Teaching and Research

Guilbert C. Hentschke

In today's global knowledge economy more organizations and individuals are paying increased attention to their intellectual property rights and obligations, especially institutions of higher education (IHEs) and their faculty (Altbach, 2015; Goh, 2009; Shields, 2013). Both pursue work as knowledge producers, consumers, and conveyers. But, which among the wide range of intellectual property (IP) issues in modern society are central to faculty and their IHEs and why? There are two approaches to these questions: first, to start from the universe of IP today and then seek to narrow the scope to the top issues affecting faculty and their institutions (Dutfield & Suthersanen, 2008); or second, to start with basic faculty work—"research" and "teaching"—and then seek their primary connections to issues of intellectual property. This chapter takes the second approach.

The approach relies on a two-by-two grid for a largely economic analysis: two broad categories of university work, "research" and "teaching" and two broad characterizations of that work that are associated with intellectual property, "commercial grade" and "educational grade" IP. Commercial grade refers to *protectionist* policies of work designed to restrict access to IP in order to seek financial gains associated with those restrictions. Educational grade refers to policies of free or very low cost *access* to IP in order to promote the spread of knowledge (a "global public good").

Faculty work can reside in all four quadrants of that matrix. (1) In the *research/commercial (northwest) quadrant* are IP protected works that seek to generate (and often have generated) major net revenues for faculty IP

New Directions for Higher Education, no. 177, Spring 2017 © 2017 Wiley Periodicals, Inc.
Published online in Wiley Online Library (wileyonlinelibrary.com) • DOI: 10.1002/he.20227

owners and their universities, such as the Gatorade IP that has brought millions of dollars to the University of Florida. (2) In the *research/educational (northeast) quadrant* are research products that both rely heavily for their creation on access to free (to the researcher) research products also have very little likelihood themselves of generating financial benefits, especially net of the costs of IP protection. (Reputational benefits may, however, accrue here.) This chapter and to a lesser extent the volume itself could fall into this quadrant, although we authors and our publisher hope it lands in one of the two commercial IP quadrants. (3) The vast majority of teaching-related products, for example, syllabi, power point lectures, pedagogical strategies, lie within the *teaching/educational (southeast) quadrant*; the monetary cost of production is very low (except for faculty time that is "prepaid" by their universities) and the market returns *to the faculty member* are usually not directly linked to the IP of a specific course. (4) In the *teaching/commercial (southwest) quadrant* we do, though, see a growing number of teaching services, which *are* both costly to produce and for which net revenues are sought, for example, some massive open online courses (MOOCs) and popular textbooks in basic, required courses. Faculty work does not fall into these four quadrants by chance, nor are the IP implications random; market characteristics of faculty work help to explain its quadrant location.

Several characteristics of the markets for university and faculty work help to explain the quadrant location of work, including how some work might gravitate from one quadrant to the other: the incremental costs of IP production; the financial and reputational risks/returns of IP production; the availability of substitutes for IP; and the viability of repurposing IP for alternative uses. The chapter concludes with a discussion of these market characteristics and their implications for faculty work.

Background: Higher Education and Intellectual Property in a Knowledge Economy

The importance of IP in higher education faculty work grows in a knowledge economy, if only because teaching and research generally increase knowledge in society. One dimension of knowledge is its intellectual property or the nature of rights to knowledge. Access to IP can be tightly restricted and protected, subject to specific limitations on its use, or freely available to all. Faculty members produce, consume, and disseminate IP—both theirs and others. IHEs in this limited framework provide opportunities for faculty to produce work, providing support to them and seeking to benefit in the financial and reputational returns from their work. IP rules and practices that govern faculty work vary among different nations but are largely uniform within a given nation (Carruthers & Halliday, 2006; Hoffman & Marcou, 1988). A nation's IP rule-making is largely recursive with repeated cycles of argument, negotiation, rule-making, implementation, enforcement, and revision (Dutfield & Suthersanen, 2008; Masnick, 2015).

Figure 6.1. Faculty Work and Intellectual Property Characteristics.

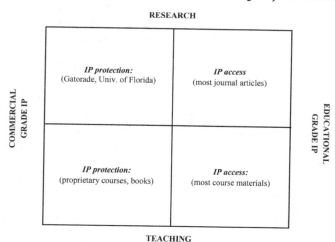

Higher education institutions have incentives to aggressively manage the "knowledge" (IP) from faculty work that they acquire, use, create, and sell. They are compelled to utilize those IP-related freedoms and protections that are available to them, if only to maintain and enhance their market position (Foray & Raffo, 2012). IHEs and their faculties are on both sides of two seemingly contradictory arguments. Arguments and rules for increasing IP *protections* are growing as the fruits of knowledge work can be monetized at scale across a global market. At the same time, rules for *access to the IP of others* is also growing as the demand for knowledge dissemination (teaching and learning) explodes across the globe.

Faculty work takes place in this larger "dynamic" and "changing" environment, fueled by forces such as rising middle classes, falling (technologically driven) costs of knowledge acquisition and transmission, continuing shifts from goods to (knowledge intensive) services and growing supplies of better skilled and more highly educated labor. For all practical purposes, however, the IP issues that affect faculty teaching and research are fairly static in the short run and are treated as such here in order to focus attention on how different kinds of research and teaching have differing market characteristics. Faculty research is somewhat more closely associated, *but not totally associated*, with IP protections. Faculty teaching is somewhat more closely associated, *but not totally associated*, with IP access. The categories are not clean, because faculty work also varies in another dimension, from work benefiting from IP protections from unauthorized use by others ("commercial grade") to work benefiting from IP rules, which provides faculty with *access* to the work of other faculty ("educational grade") and vice versa. See Figure 6.1.

New Directions for Higher Education • DOI: 10.1002/he

IP rules, for both protection and access, are both a cause and a result of economic activity: it is hard to tell when changes in markets for goods and services affect IP policies and practices and when changes in IP policies and practices affect markets for goods and services. Growth in economic development and IP protections have been uneven, varying not just by region (developed versus developing parts of the world), but also by industrial sector, and are found especially among knowledge intensive industries such as genomics and digital technology, and in places hospitable to them, such as Singapore (Baber, 2008; Fai & Morgan, 2007), and Silicon Valley. Arguments for IP *access*, on the other hand, are more in evidence in regions and communities where basic knowledge via schooling is most in demand and least in evidence. Both protection and access arguments address different markets and different knowledge products, and often, different people. This applies as much to faculty work *within* a single university as it does to regions of the world.

The value of different work products varies greatly, both economically and in noneconomic terms. Teaching differs from research, not just in terms of "transmitted" versus "created" knowledge. For many faculty, teaching duties are assigned and course descriptions are listed in the school's bulletin. Faculty need access to up-to-date resources (other people's IP) in order to create and present a credible course, and most institutions make those available through their libraries at no cost to the faculty member. For these same faculty, conducting a program of research is entirely another matter. In theory, the time and IP necessary to invent and carry out a program of research are also made available to the faculty member, but it is largely up to the faculty member to organize (and financially support) his or her program of research. Faculty "programs of research" vary greatly in quality, quantity, impact, and perceived value. Teaching loads, in contrast, are largely similar across faculty: variations in perceived teaching value—both reputational and monetary—are narrow relative to variations in perceived research value.

What passes for research in IHEs, then, varies in material ways. Some research is costly to produce and would not be produced absent some subsidy or possible return on investment. Examples include research requiring technologically advanced laboratories. Other IP has virtually no chance of garnering *economic* returns to faculty, but gets produced anyway, partly because it costs so little to produce and is an expected part of most faculty work. In addition, the possible *reputational* benefits of the resulting IP may enhance faculty motivation to undertake research. Examples include articles in peer-reviewed journals and even academic books. Economic returns are often not sufficient, by themselves, to warrant producing a given research article, but reputational measures often more than compensate. Reputational benefits can also foster long-run economic benefits resulting from merit raises, promotions, or more lucrative job offers. IP rules of copyright and citation support access to IP (a public good argument), and also act to enhance the reputation of the faculty member producing that IP.

The general IP issue associated with faculty work is not so much whether to pursue protection or access in the abstract. Rather, the issue arises "naturally" from the concrete characteristics of the work itself. Some research and teaching benefits from IP protection, and other research and teaching benefits from free access to IP; and some benefit from both. These generalizations about faculty work are characterized in Figure 6.1, especially in the northwest and southeast quadrants. Faculty engaged in commercial grade/research (northwest) tend to produce IP that is relatively high cost and aimed at future returns on investments. Faculty engaged in educational grade/teaching tend to produce IP that is relatively low cost and for which there is relatively low economic or reputational returns. The reputational returns from students who love the class and its instructor are very important to some faculty and to their IHEs, but such reputational returns seldom extend to the entire campus, not to mention beyond it. The reputational benefits of "good" teaching are more localized than the reputational benefits of "good" research. Nonetheless, these benefits are often still sufficient to entice some faculty members to produce a terrific course.

The distinctions among the quadrants are more a matter of degree, not of kind, and are reflected especially in the southwest and northeast quadrants. Educational grade faculty research has little association with economic returns. Certainly more costly research in this quadrant is subsidized by grants from a faculty member's institution, foundations, or government agencies, but seldom if ever is this research produced with the expectation of monetization. Faculty owners of this IP do seek to have it easily accessed by others, spread widely, and to be acknowledged as its creators. At the same time, some educational work does have commercial value (southwest quadrant) and IP protections facilitate that. As higher education continues to grow globally, IP policies and practices (both for protection and access) will emerge in importance (Raduntz, 2005) for a variety of reasons (Gurry & Halbert, 2005) and at most colleges and universities.

Currently, however, increases in aggregate demands for *access* to IP appear to be outpacing increases in demands for increased *protections* of IP, largely because in the aggregate, the teaching work of faculty in higher education (especially in the southeast quadrant) is growing faster than research work (especially in the northwest quadrant). Individual faculty members can locate their work across the quadrants; and the quadrant location of that work in part defines how a given faculty member is viewed by his or her IHE. Before addressing this in depth, though, it is necessary to examine the market characteristics of faculty work across these quadrants, especially vis-à-vis widely differing IHEs. Individual faculty members vary greatly in the degree to which they are or seek to be "research active," "largely teaching," or one of many other characterizations. The same labels are attached to individual IHEs. How do institutions support (or constrain) faculty members as they produce IP in the different quadrants? How does institutional support of faculty work in the northwest quadrant (commercial grade IP in research) differ from its support for faculty work in the southeast quadrant (educational grade IP in teaching)?

IP Protection for Commercial Grade Research—For Society's Benefit

University-based commercial grade IP is created, protected, and monetized through "technology transfer," a term describing the university infrastructure surrounding its IP protection. Tech transfer produces benefits to society at large, as argued by its primary, largely university-based, trade group, the Association of University Technology Managers (AUTM):

> Technology transfer moves ideas from research institutions to the marketplace *to improve the quality of life and benefit society*. Technology transfer offices assist the efforts of researchers to identify commercially viable technologies and obtain patents or other legal protection for the intellectual property ... [and] also help promote these technologies to potential licensees, negotiate licensing agreements and manage their respective institution's portfolio of licenses and patents. Licensees—from startups to large companies—are typically responsible for commercializing the licensed technologies by integrating the technologies into products and overseeing the development, manufacture and marketing of those products. The patenting of discoveries is fundamental to attracting companies, entrepreneurs and investors into allocating the necessary resources to ensure that these discoveries have the opportunity to reach the stream of commerce. The returns on this investment are the products that benefit the public, drive economic growth and employment, and generate state and federal tax revenues. *These technology transfer efforts are pursued in concert with the research institutions' core values of sharing research results, materials and know-how for the betterment of the community and society.* (emphases added) (AUTM, 2014, p. 10)

The 200 plus U.S. IHEs—or more accurately, a small subset of faculty within this small subset of IHEs—aggressively pursue commercial grade IP that currently generate more than $65B in total research expenditures, nearly two-thirds of which emanates from agencies of the federal government and nearly one-tenth of which emanates from industry sources (AUTM, 2014, p. 12). The "pipeline" of research money fuels the creation of research leading to IP protections such as patents. These IHEs spend in excess of $500M annually in legal fees to file in excess of 40K patents, while nearly 6K patents are issued from filings in previous years (AUTM, 2014, p. 71). The costs of IP protection and enforcement are borne within the framework of expected economic and reputational benefits that accrue to these research universities. The IP "pipeline" passes via various forms of licensing arrangements into business enterprises, including both startups and established businesses, both domestic and foreign. The "protection" characteristics of IP are centrally located here, at the *transition* from university (with its general culture of open access information) to business enterprise (with its profit-seeking, proprietary culture) (Mars & Rios-Aguilar, 2010). In 2013, more than 43K licenses and options were filed, of which more than 5K licenses and more than 1K options were executed, plus nearly 500 more containing equity (AUTM, p. 6).

These economic indicia of IP represent the proverbial tip of the iceberg. Following from this pipeline is a flow of new commercial products and a proliferation and growth of firms producing these goods, both domestically and internationally (Hagedoorn, Cloodt, & van Kranenburg, 2005; Madhavan & Iriyama, 2009), with variations in IP protections across borders (Reichman & Dreyfuss, 2007; Samuelson, 2004). For illustration, per one estimate of university IP domestic economic impact on biotech industries alone from 1996 to 2010 was "as much as $388B on U.S. GDP and $836B on U.S. gross industrial output, ... creating as many as 3M jobs" (AUTM, 2014, p. 8). In addition, revenues from recurring fees to both IHEs and their principal investigators represent a separate, smaller, form of monetary impact. Nondomestic impact would further add to these measures.

The vast majority of what falls under the label of university (and faculty) research is *not* commercial grade as described above. Rather, it is produced at relatively low incremental cost, has a variety of near substitutes, and usually generates little incremental economic or commercial value, other than that which flows indirectly from the added reputational value of the researcher/producer. In effect, noncommercial grade university research resembles educational grade IP (Figure 6.1 and discussed later) more than it resembles commercial-grade IP.

IP Access for Educational Grade Teaching—For Society's Benefit

IP *access* is intrinsic to the production of instructional grade knowledge products at universities, just as IP *protection* is intrinsic to the production of commercial grade knowledge products. With low-cost access to the IP of others through "fair" or "classroom" use provisions in copyright law (U.S. Copyright Office, 2016), IHE faculties assemble and produce course offerings that fulfill their contractual obligations to their employer-universities, which IHEs in turn seek to monetize through instructional offerings that they sell to students. For the vast majority of IHEs and their faculties, teaching is the primary service delivered. Courses and programs are bundled into degrees and sold to students. The "raw materials" for these courses are drawn from freely available knowledge products housed in university-supported libraries and nonuniversity digital media. The incremental "cost" to a faculty member of acquisition, use and production of instructional IP involves citation of its source, which, net of professor time, is close to zero; the major costs of instructional grade IP have already been incurred by the institution and made freely available to individual faculty members to support their scholarly teaching and writing.

Simply stated, faculty are hired, and they create and offer courses, which are sold to students. In fact, however, a more realistic understanding of the production and infrastructure requirements for pursuit of instructional grade IP would include libraries, classrooms, marketing, and delivery technologies. Libraries (electronic and physical) represent a fundamental component of educational grade IP. These costs are paid for by universities and made available at no cost to faculty for their use. Faculty members draw from—and contribute to—this pool of low cost (to them) IP. IHEs then seek to produce educational grade IP and then monetize it, just like they seek to produce commercial grade IP and then monetize it. Institutions seek to recoup their investment in teaching by selling courses to students; their provision of "free" educational grade IP to faculty is a necessary and real cost to the IHEs that employ them.

The arguments on behalf of greater educational grade IP access, like those on behalf of commercial grade IP protection, are broadly portrayed as pursuing a global public good. These arguments reflect those associated specifically with the Open Education Resources movement (discussed in greater detail in other chapters). Open Education Resources (OER) are teaching and learning materials freely available for everyone to use, whether you are a teacher or a learner. This includes full courses, modules, syllabi, lectures, homework assignments, quizzes, lab activities, pedagogical materials, games, simulations, and many more resources contained in digital media collections from around the world OER. The societal benefits of OER and instructional grade IP follow from prior arguments asserting the public goods benefits of *education*, as reflected in the preamble to UNESCO's "2012 Paris Declaration" supporting the growth of OER in the world:

> Mindful of relevant international statements including: The Universal Declaration of Human Rights (Article 26.1), which states that: "*Everyone has the right to education*"; The International Covenant on Economic, Social and Cultural Rights (Article 13.1), which recognizes "the *right of everyone to education*"; The 1971 Berne Convention for the Protection of Literary and Artistic Works and the 1996 WIPO Copyright Treaty; The Millennium Declaration and the 2000 Dakar Framework for Action, which made global commitments to provide quality basic education for *all children, youth and adults*; The 2003 World Summit on the Information Society, Declaration of Principles, committing "to build a people centered, inclusive and development-oriented Information Society *where everyone can create, access, utilize and share information and knowledge*." (emphasis added) (UNESCO, 2012)

The implication is straightforward: free access to knowledge products fosters the growth of knowledge (through education), and the resulting positive benefits accrue from that to "everyone." This public good argument for (free) educational grade IP is independent of the public good arguments supporting commercial grade IP protection, which are by definition more focused on (limited to) those individuals who benefit from the production of commercial grade IP products, such as Allegra and Lyrica (and Gatorade) discussed earlier.

Why Does Faculty Work "Fall" Into Differing Quadrants?

Differences between commercial grade IP and educational grade IP involves more than differences between R&D labs with researchers producing commercial grade IP on the one hand and classrooms with instructors producing educational grade IP on the other. Rather, the primary difference lies in the different market-related qualities of the IP itself. Educational grade IP costs little to produce, has few risks or rewards associated with its production, has a wide variety of substitutes, and can't be easily repurposed (i.e., used by others for a novel application). In sum, it is very difficult to monetize. Commercial grade IP, on the other hand, is expensive to produce, has few if any substitutes, and can be readily repurposed and (hopefully) monetized.

Low Incremental Costs of Educational IP Production. Costs associated with producing an additional course are relatively low, regardless of whether it is offered for the first time or is an updated version of an existing course. The costs of course-related reading materials are either passed on to students or accessed at virtually no incremental cost from the digital archives of IHE libraries. Textbooks associated with courses are protected from unlimited copying, although subsections can be copied, cited, and made available for "classroom use." At the same time, and with 21st-century developments in instructional technology and free/low-cost digital resources, required readings for courses are increasingly free to faculty and students. (Arguments about the high costs of course delivery are associated more with tuition pricing strategies of IHEs than with actual costs associated with course production.) The *sum total* of educational IP is large, but this aggregate is extremely granular—most courses are produced independently of each other by individual faculty members. Individual courses are added, dropped, modified, combined with other courses, and recombined without directly affecting other courses, let alone the overall instructional processes of IHEs. Courses and faculty publications are largely produced by individual faculty members. In both cases, individual faculty producing instructional grade IP seek access to the IP of others at virtually no cost to them, and in turn their prospects for realizing substantial financial gains from their instructional grade IP are very low. Alternatively, reputational gains can be substantial and provide sufficient incentives to produce educational IP (Doctorow, 2014).

Low Risks Associated With Educational IP Production. Producing educational grade IP also presents a low financial risk to faculty, because

their IHEs have assumed the financial risks associated with low course enrollments and mediocre student reviews. Short-run compensation is not at
risk. The same can be said for financial risks associated with producing
educational grade research. IHEs often indirectly reward this faculty work
within their annual compensation schemes (larger raises and chances of
promotion with more publications), but IHE and faculty benefits are mostly
"reputational" rather than "monetary."

In contrast, commercial grade IP is associated with the high cost of
production, high reputational returns, and potentially high financial return
coupled with potentially high risk of failure. Both IHEs and their faculty can
gain both reputation and money in producing commercial grade IP, but it
is by no means certain. IHEs often assume high start-up costs in producing
commercial grade IP, and in return agree on a percentage of any financial
returns that come from licensing (protected) IP.

Educational IP and Availability of a Wide Variety of Substitutes.
Free and nearly free e-resources provide substitutes for course texts, but
also for courses themselves. More generally, however, courses from different
IHEs are becoming substitutes for each other. Differences across IHEs in the
content of "Economics 101" and other basic courses are much smaller than
similarities. Whether through homogenization or standardization, similar
course labels increasingly reflect similar content, regardless of institutional
differences. There is some evidence of this also happening globally and at
the degree level (Goh, 2009). Increasingly students transfer courses into
programs at IHEs, transfer across IHEs to complete programs, and move
across borders as they consume instruction. Finally, most IHEs are growing its suite of programs and creating (subdegree and postdegree) certificate programs in efforts to attract students. The "bundled" IP of many IHEs
is unbundling. Even "university brand" is seeing not so much erosion as
diversification and proliferation (Craig, 2015). Non-IHEs, especially large
technology-related corporations, are entering higher education, selling their
instructional grade IP in the student marketplace. From both a producer
(IHE) and a consumer (student) perspective, a growing array of instructional grade IP *substitutes* is available. Ready access to substitutes places
downward pressure on the economic value of educational grade IP and the
viability of protecting it.

Educational IP and its Repurposing Viability.   Courses created and
taught by one faculty member are not readily suited to be "sold" to and
then taught by another faculty member at another institution. Although
the market-making capabilities of the Internet increase the theoretical likelihood of such transactions, it is difficult to imagine incentives that would
significantly increase either the supply or demand for course syllabi. There
are, however, two categories of faculty-developed educational grade IP
that do have some potential repurposing viability and could be of value
to others: commercially successful books and completely packaged (self-
contained) online courses. Commercially successful books, for example,

Paul Samuelson's *Economics*, can serve a variety of purposes other than be the required text for economics 101. Similarly, a self-contained online instructional package could be reused and offered by other faculty, for other courses, and at other institutions. Unlike individual courses, these IP products require greater amounts of investment capital (from the publisher or the university) to produce and might find their way into secondary markets, raising the possibility of conflicting claims over those revenues (Noble, 1998) and the protections afforded by current IP rules and practices. (Can an IHE use or sell an online course developed by a faculty member without compensating her or him?) These and other examples of commercial grade/teaching IP tend to exist when it is in unusually large demand and cannot be imitated at low cost. Universities and their faculties negotiate percentage shares of the proceeds from commercial grade IP and have largely left to the faculty any of the relatively few proceeds from instructional grade IP such as textbooks.

Commercial Grade IP, Educational Grade IP, and Implications for Faculty

Aggregate demand for both types of IHE-generated IP is growing, but their markets are quite different. Globally, enrollments in higher education are rapidly growing, fueling demand for educational grade IP. Low costs of course and program production, external subsidies, and effective prices together shape IHE teaching. The market for courses continues to grow, but as consumers of an "experience good," students are not in a position to comparison shop similar courses across institutions. They are generally limited to the courses offered at *their* individual institutions. At the same time, institutions vary greatly in their offerings and the prices they charge: some have significant pricing power and others have none. The degree to which an IHE can then monetize its educational grade IP varies greatly, depending on the demands of its student market. It is unrealistic for most institutions and their faculty members to place "big bets" on most educational IP products, given its typical characteristics (production costs, risks, substitutability, and repurposing potential).

Demand for educational grade IP differs from demand for commercial grade IP in that student markets for the former are much more segmented, fragmented, and produced and consumed in small units (degrees) by individuals who face multiple substitutes. Markets for the latter, in contrast, operate with a relatively small number of corporate producers who use (repurpose) commercial grade IP into products for which there are no practical substitutes. Those producers compete to create and sell the fruits of commercial grade IP products into (potentially) global markets. IHEs—and their faculty members—that pursue research resulting in the production of commercial grade IP are expecting, at least hoping for, economic returns commensurate with their investments.

Pressures to globalize both IP protections and IP access across universities are spreading, but they run the risk of being conflated. On occasion, all IP has been lumped together as "knowledge," and the impact of IP protections on "the global public good" is contested. In effect, arguments on behalf of educational grade IP have been levied against commercial grade IP, especially when IP is framed as a fundamental adjunct to neoliberal economic policy (Salokannel, 2003). These arguments flow from the argument made by Joseph Stiglitz and others that knowledge is a public good, indeed a *global* public good (Stiglitz, 1999). The implications of this are that, separate from "transmission costs," knowledge can remain free and that, with limited exceptions, no one can be excluded from using knowledge. This argument has been built on by others to characterize the harmful (nonpublic good) dimensions of IP regimes, to wit:

> The more valuable knowledge becomes as a means of production, the more pervasive is its commodification, extending to ever new realms of knowledge. Different forms of knowledge are more and more privatized and subjugated to private property rights. In case of knowledge-assets this means intellectual property rights, in particular copyrights and patents . . . . The counterpart of this phenomenon is access to knowledge. The more knowledge is commodified and subject to private ownership, the more access to knowledge is restricted. This in its turn entails the *division of the world* to *those who have* access to knowledge and consequently, to further production of knowledge on the one hand, and to *those who do not have* the means to access the growing knowledge stocks. (emphasis added) (Salokannel, 2003, p. 351)

The author is arguing in effect that excessive commercial grade IP, through its protectionist features, is depriving large portions of humanity of the fruits of IP that is being protected.

As consumers and producers of knowledge services (research and teaching), IHEs and their faculty members are necessarily included as agents in this argument, but the argument seems incomplete, even selective. Both the private and the public benefits of postsecondary education, through the creation of educational grade IP, have been widely documented and accepted. This is largely the result of its teaching mission and creation of educational grade IP, and access to this IP does foster societal benefits, à la Stiglitz's argument. At the same time, at least two categories of beneficiaries of university-based research and development of commercial grade IP need to be recognized as well. One includes the direct beneficiaries of IP end products, such as the people who are aided by taking Allegra and Lyrica. A second set includes all who work along the IP pipeline making a living, and contributing to society, as they help bring those products to market. Many others, of course, do not benefit as directly, such as those who cannot afford IP end products and those who do not have access to them due to IP restrictions on new, low-cost producers.

NEW DIRECTIONS FOR HIGHER EDUCATION • DOI: 10.1002/he

Regardless of personal inclinations on the IP issues of protection and access, all IHEs and their faculties operate *within* an existing IP web in all of its local, national, and global intricacy and variability. The implications of that IP web for faculty work depends primarily on the nature of characteristics of their work. At the extremes, faculty working on commercial grade IP at a "research university" in a highly educated region in a "developed country" will be more concerned with IP protections; faculty developing educational grade IP as an instructor in a "struggling college" with an "instructional mission" in an "emerging economy" will be more concerned with access to the IP of others (Teferra & Altbach, 2004). In the second depiction, more fundamental national issues act to reduce the likelihood of faculty members conducting research that results in commercial grade IP— funding, privatization, government functioning, compulsory school system pipeline, institutional governance, gender issues, language issues, technology infrastructure, brain drain, and the rule of law, among others (Spring, 2009).

IP-fostered economic development in knowledge-intensive fields, then, is not so much *kept out of* less developed nations and their IHEs as it is *attracted to* "regions that have innovative firms, government laboratories and universities," sometimes referred to as "agglomeration effects" (Niosi & Bas, 2001). Commercial grade IP grows only in a few IHEs and only as other conditions exist, such as a sufficiency of highly educated researchers in a region. They may grow in developing IHEs, but only over a longer time horizon. Implications for individual faculty members and their work follow directly from this: most faculty will produce educational grade IP through their teaching and research. A relatively small fraction of all faculty will produce commercial grade IP in the process of doing their research and teaching, partly because most IHEs do not support that type of faculty work and partly because faculty are either disinclined or not qualified.

At a more granular level, the implications of IP trends for higher education faculty are multiple and increasingly difficult to capture within a single framework, especially given the multiple missions of higher education and the inherent specialization of faculty work. The three basic missions associated with most IHEs—teaching, research, and service—provide a first-order basis for understanding higher education's *differing and diverging* IP trends in a global knowledge economy. Of the three IHE missions, teaching dominates and is growing. Much that is described as research has little monetizing potential; only a tiny fraction of faculty are engaged in producing commercial grade IP, although the monetary impact is disproportionately large.

As they expand to serve larger numbers and proportions of society, IHEs collectively are increasingly considered more as "means," providing human capital for employers, and less so "ends," that is, directly addressing large problems in society. Pursuit of ambitious "ends" through large-scale research and development requires human, financial, and social capital available to relatively few IHEs (hundreds among thousands) (McClure, 2014), whereas programs of teaching, educating students for future work, is provided by virtually all, even the most modestly equipped IHEs. Although teaching and research are usually intentionally conflated on the presumption that "good" teaching is informed by research, the IP implications of each are at odds. Individual faculty are often encouraged to conduct research in their area of specialization, but the aggregate commercial value of such research is usually small relative to the reputational value that accrues to the faculty member. Faculty will be increasingly interested in IP frameworks (both protection and access), only when those frameworks materially affect the quality and monetization of their work.

References

Altbach, P. (2015, Spring). Massification and the global knowledge economy: The continuing contradiction. *International Higher Education*, (80), 4.

Association of University Technology Managers. (2014). *Highlights of AUTM's U.S. licensing activity survey, FY2013*, p. 10. Retrieved from http://www.autm.net/AUTMMain/media/Resources/Documents/AUTM_US_Highlights_FY2013_no_Data_Appendix.pdf

Baber, Z. (2008). Global DNA: Genomics, the nation-state and globalisation. *Asian Journal of Social Science*, 36(1). Special Focus: State, Culture and the Economy, 104–119.

Carruthers, B., & Halliday, T. (2006, Summer). Negotiating globalization: Global scripts and intermediation in the construction of Asian insolvency regimes, *Law & Social Inquiry*, 31(3), 521–584.

Craig, R. (2015). *College disrupted: The great unbundling of higher education*. New York NY: Palgrave MacMillan.

Doctorow, C. (2014). *Information doesn't want to be free: Laws for the internet age*. San Francisco, CA: McSweeney's.

Dutfield, G., & Suthersanen, U. (2008). *Global intellectual property law*. Cheltenham, UK: Edward Elgar.

Fai, F., & Morgan, E. (2007). Innovation, competition and regulatory change: Assessing interrelationships at the industry level. *MIR: Management International Review*, 47(5), Innovation, Competition and Change in International Business, 767–785.

Foray, D., & Raffo, J. (2012). Business-driven innovation: Is it making a difference in education? An Analysis of Educational Patents, *OECD Education Working Papers*, (84), OECD Publishing. http://dx.doi.org/10.1787/5k91dl7pc835-en

Goh, Wee Pin, J. (2009, August). Globalization's culture consequences of MBA education across Australia and Singapore: Sophistry or truth? *Higher Education*, 58(2), 131–155.

Gurry, F., & Halbert, D. (2005, March 30–April 2). Globalization, development, and intellectual property: New challenges and new opportunities. *Proceedings of the Annual Meeting. American Society of International Law*, 99, 291–300.

Hagedoorn, J., Cloodt, D., & van Kranenburg, H. (2005, March). Intellectual property rights and the governance of international partnerships. *Journal of International Business Studies*, 36(2), 175–186.

Hoffman, G. M., & Marcou, G. T. (1988, September). Intellectual property right issues in the new trade bill. *Technology and Society Magazine, IEEE*, 7(3), 4, 8.

Madhavan, R., & Iriyama, A. (2009, October–November). Understanding global flows of venture capital: Human networks as the "Carrier Wave" of globalization. *Journal of International Business Studies*, 40(8), 1241–1259.

Mars, M., & Rios-Aguilar, C. (2010, April). Academic entrepreneurship (re) defined: Significance and implications for the scholarship of higher education. *Higher Education, 59*(4), 441–460.

Masnick, M. (2015). Congress finally releases fast track trade bill, and it's a mess. *TechDirt.* Retrieved from https://www.techdirt.com/articles/20150416/13475530676/congress-finally-releases-fast-track-trade-bill-mess.shtml

McClure, M. W. (2014). MOOCs, wicked problems, and the spirit of the liberal arts. *The Journal of General Education, 63*(4), 269–286.

Niosi, J., & Bas, T. G. (2001, August–September). The competencies of regions: Canada's clusters in biotechnology. *Small Business Economics, 17*(1–2), 31–42.

Noble, D. F. (1998). Digital diploma mills, Part II: The coming battle over online instruction. *Sociological Perspectives, 41*(4), 815–825.

Raduntz, H. (2005). The marketization of education within the global capitalist economy. In M. W. Apple, J. Kenway, & M. Singh (Eds.), *Globalizing education: Policies, pedagogies, and politics* (pp. 231–245). New York, NY: Peter Lang.

Reichman, J. H., & Cooper Dreyfuss, R. (2007, October). Harmonization without consensus: Critical reflections on drafting a substantive patent law treaty. *Duke Law Journal, 57*(1), 85–130.

Salokannel, M. (2003, October). Global public goods and private rights: Scientific research and intellectual property rights. *Nordiskt Immateriellt Rättskydd, 4,* 334–358.

Samuelson, P. (2004, Winter). Intellectual property arbitrage: How foreign rules can affect domestic protections. *The University of Chicago Law Review, 71*(1), 223–239.

Shields, R. (2013, November). Globalization and international student mobility: A network analysis. *Comparative Education Review, 57*(4), 609–636.

Spring, J. (2009). *Globalization of education: An introduction.* New York, NY: Routledge.

Stiglitz, J. E. (1999). Knowledge as a global public good. In Kaul, Inge, I. Grunberg, & M. A. Stern (Eds.), *Global public goods: International cooperation in the 21st century.* New York, NY: Oxford University Press.

Teferra, D., & Altbach, P. G. (2004, January). African higher education: Challenges for the 21st century. *Higher Education, 47*(1), 21–50.

UNESCO. (2012). *Paris OER declaration.* Retrieved from http://www.unesco.org/new/fileadmin/MULTIMEDIA/HQ/CI/CI/pdf/Events/English_Paris_OER_Declaration.pdf

United States Copyright Office. (2016). *Circular 21, reproduction of copyrighted works by educators and librarians.* Retrieved October 3, 2016, from http://copyright.gov/circs/

GUILBERT C. HENTSCHKE *is senior advisor, Parthenon-EY, and Stoops Dean and Cooper Chair Emeritus, University of Southern California's Rossier School of Education.*

7

This chapter synthesizes the previous chapters to offer to readers practical recommendations for navigating IP issues, including resources and advice for faculty and administrations to engage in more equitable discussions about the rights of faculty and the interests of the public good.

Faculty Voice in Intellectual Property Policies: Collective Action for the Public Good

Adrianna Kezar

There are paradoxical tensions emerging for faculty members. On the one hand, groups like the American Association of University Professors (AAUP) are calling for faculty to defend their rights to intellectual property (IP) as campuses increasingly are infringing on once honored IP rights among faculty. As institutions seek to profit from faculty IP, groups are calling faculty to defend what has historically been the right to assert ownership over their own IP that results as part of their scholarly work in teaching and research. In issuing its 2013 report—*Defending the Freedom to Innovate: Faculty Intellectual Property Rights After Stanford v. Roche*—the AAUP called for institutions to work more with faculty leaders on campus to design their policies around IP and to develop arrangements that support both individual faculty rights and institutional IP rights, where appropriate. The report notes how faculty rights have been muted in recent years, compared to institutional rights, where faculty create IP using any institutional resources or facilities.

So while on the one hand faculty are being called to fight for their IP rights, there are also forces asking them to support an openness movement that would make their IP part of the public realm. Some scholars have labeled this tension a hybrid identity or ethical stance—compelling faculty to consider a complex set of issues that are unchartered with values that sometimes compete (McSherry, 2001). But both views relate to the notion that institutions are overreaching in their claims to faculty's IP and that faculty should be able to make the decision about how their IP is used—whether to profit from it (through licensing or patents) or make it available to the public.

New Directions for Higher Education, no. 177, Spring 2017 © 2017 Wiley Periodicals, Inc.
Published online in Wiley Online Library (wileyonlinelibrary.com) • DOI: 10.1002/he.20228

The changing legal (see Badke's chapter in this volume) and social/economic landscape due to the rise of academic capitalism (noted in several chapters) and the ensuing lack of historical consensus about faculty rights over their IP suggests we are at an important crossroads in which stakeholders in higher education need to be brought into discussion about IP rights. Faculty need to take collective action to reassert their own place in discussions on this issue. Because of the long tradition of faculty rights on which there was for so long a consensus, faculty members have not felt the need to negotiate or take action on this issue.

Unfortunately, faculty collective action around IP rights has not been forthcoming. Yet the recent rise of unionization among adjunct faculty and the greater recognition of faculty rights being eroded away—generally—may lead to a much stronger collective response from faculty in coming years. Such efforts can be supported by the AAUP, which has drafted a statement on IP and created a toolkit for faculty. The AAUP has also issued a guide to academic–industry relationships to inform campus efforts in this area, a statement on copyright, a statement on distance education and faculty rights, and case letters. Case letters were written to address specific IP issues when faculty members feel their rights have been violated by administrative decisions on campuses. Faculty have to contend against significant institutional interests as major associations such as the National Association of College and University Attorneys (NACUA), have made significant arguments for why institutions should own faculty IP if they use any institutional resources. Publishers, industry partners, and technology companies partnering for online courses all have their own institutional interests that they are asserting that are meant to be privileged above faculty interests.

Interestingly, these IP concerns are not only an issue for faculty. Institutions are extending their IP rights reach over staff and students as well. Ohio State University's IP language is an example of this type of overreach among campuses. Their recent proposal noted that all IP created by faculty, staff, and students belongs to Ohio State if it were made under any of these criteria: under the scope of OSU employment; using university infrastructure, money or equipment; or in a university research laboratory. Such language is so broad that any IP created by a member of the academic community would be owned by the institution. The University of Berkeley presents another case of this overreach where administrators signed a contract with MIT/edX without consultation with faculty that set up a series of online courses where faculty who teach in the programs sign away their rights to IP to their courses. These new courses are not treated as the other courses throughout the system, which are protected by IP rights.

Most commentators grant that optional agreements that are developed in terms of tasks for hire can be developed between faculty and institutions. However, most of the disagreement today is the overreach of administrators

NEW DIRECTIONS FOR HIGHER EDUCATION • DOI: 10.1002/he

asserting their rights over faculty IP that takes place as a part of their normal scholarship and teaching that many believe should continue to be protected under faculty IP rights. Many campuses are unilaterally changing policies and stripping faculty of their rights, which critics comment is problematic.

On occasion, national organizations develop policy statements related to IP, such as the American Council on Education's *Developing a Distance Education Policy for the 21st Century*, or the Association of American Universities' *Intellectual Property and New Media Technologies: A Framework for Development at AAU Institutions*. However, these are typically aimed at protecting the interests of campuses among external vendors that may try to usurp the IP of faculty/institutions. Interestingly, the institutions do not see the irony in their need to protect themselves against external organizations that assert rights over faculty IP when the institutions themselves are also engaged in this behavior.

Collective Negotiation of Professional Autonomy and Managerial Discretion: The Need for Collective Action

Many of the chapters in this volume have brought up the issue of returning to a more transparent environment in which administrators negotiate rights with faculty rather than the recent history of managerial discretion and assertion of authority where policies are changed with little or no faculty input. Faculty mobilization is likely to aid in rebalancing power between faculty and their administrations. Certain efforts toward collective action have already helped to establish some middle ground between faculty and their institutions as it relates to IP. But we need more faculty to join such efforts.

In order for faculty rights to be asserted, faculty members will need to work through national organizations and with others on campus to come up against these powerful interests. Although faculty members can use the ideas in this monograph to be more savvy in their own employment contracts and in examining contracts that they sign with publishers, industry, or campuses related to their IP, there are many ways that faculty can work collectively to support their rights.

Disciplinary societies are increasingly establishing subcommittees and statements on IP. For example, the Modern Languages Association has a toolkit and portion of their website devoted to issues around IP. Faculty unions have been able to negotiate strong language in support of faculty IP rights and, as noted in Rhoades' chapter, are a source for language and policy to better support faculty rights in IP. In addition to advice offered in Rhoades' chapter, unions have created toolkits, noted above, and additional resources on how faculty can support their rights (Smith, Dougherty, & Rhoades, 2011).

NEW DIRECTIONS FOR HIGHER EDUCATION • DOI: 10.1002/he

National reports and white papers are currently being developed by many different faculty groups. Rather than re-creating the wheel, individual faculty members and groups supporting faculty (such as faculty senates and unions) can access well-researched reports and concept papers on issues of faculty rights to inform campus decision making and to consider their own individual contract negotiations. For example, the California State University system academic affairs committee created a white paper related to online education and IP (2012) that examines their own policies but puts it in the context of broader policies nationally and develops recommendations for better supporting faculty rights including contingent faculty. Papers such as this are also available online, making them easy tools to access and use.

Librarians are becoming expert mediators in the world of openness and online education and can become helpful allies to faculty. Faculty groups should work more with librarians as they share interests in making scholarship available at low costs. Additionally, librarians often have much more expertise on these issues as they impact their day-to-day work decisions and environment.

Increasingly, campuses are creating committees and task forces related to IP. Unfortunately, faculty with knowledge about the administrative overreach are often not included in these groups. In addition, these committees are often not given significant visibility, preventing concerns from being registered. Faculty members can support improved collective action by raising the visibility of these committees, ensuring that faculty across campus are involved in discussions, and if committees and groups are established to examine the IP language in faculty handbooks, it is important that such groups explore the language adopted by national groups supporting faculty IP rights. We also need ways to intervene on the increasing number of partnership agreements with outside groups to deliver distance education that have significant IP implications that often are governed outside traditional shared governance arrangements. Administrators claim they need quick decisions, and so they unilaterally act on these arrangements, circumventing the typical campus governance system. Faculty need to assert their interests in these decisions.

Examples of Middle Ground to Build On

Collective action, while rare, may be increasing. Occasional meetings have occurred that include faculty and administrators, such as the Network for Academic Renewal of the American Association of Colleges and Universities, which discussed faculty involvement in technology and IP issues. Several disciplinary societies and groups have held similar gatherings, such as the National Initiative for the networked cultural heritage by the College of Art Association.

As stakeholders come together, there are some good examples of language that support both faculty and institutional rights around IP. For example, the California Faculty Association has insured as a part of the collective bargaining agreement the following language:

> Article 39 of the Collective Bargaining Agreement covers faculty intellectual property rights. The article assures faculty retain the rights to materials they create, as long as there is no "extraordinary University support" in creating those materials.

> The contract expands the list of materials taking into account more contemporary and electronic works including those developed for online delivery. The list of protected materials in Article 39.3 includes, "... *works that are used in connection with online or hybrid instruction, transmitted electronically, and/or stored on CSU or third party provided servers.*"

It further stipulates that, "... Unless there is a separate agreement to the contrary, consistent with this Article, neither the CSU nor third party providers are entitled to grant licenses or make assignments with respect to such materials to publishers and publishing agents, or any third party."

This type of language protects the more generic IP created as part of faculties' scholarly and teaching work, and clearly articulates that faculty would need to use extraordinary institutional support or resources for institutions to have a claim to their IP. Given the recent overreach of administrative groups, it is important that faculty groups share language that is created to establish more of a middle ground that supports faculty rights.

Environment of Academic Capitalism

Each chapter in this volume describes how higher education leaders have become entrenched in a logic of academic capitalism and how this has led to the overreach by administrators to faculty IP rights. As alluded to earlier, studies of IP policies show that institutions have included a much longer list of exemptions to faculty owning their IP, so what was a mostly automatic ownership policy for faculty is increasingly subject to interpretation, and the long list of exceptions makes areas or territories murky (Loggie et al., 2007; Packard, 2002). Some universities, some faculty, and even some students have increased their personal wealth by asserting ownership of the IP created at the university. Because of these incentives and rewards, the academic capitalist ethic is becoming more and more entrenched in individual psyches and work.

As funding for research and education become tighter, McSherry (2001) argued, entrepreneurial attitudes challenge traditional collegial attitudes toward knowledge sharing and are subtly rewriting the unspoken rules of academic behavior. For many faculty, however, this new entrepreneurial orientation runs deeply counter to traditions of education and public service. Past campus debates about aspects of this cultural shift have created an environment of distrust and rancor. I believe the anti-entrepreneurial attitudes McSherry described have spilled over into faculty attitudes toward the use of digital technologies for teaching. But the forces of academic capitalism mean faculty are wrestling with competing values that put them in contradictory and awkward positions.

Public Good?

It is still hard to understand what is in the best interest of the public good as it relates to faculty IP. Could a fully open environment lead to a decline in innovation among faculty? Bernstein-Sierra's chapter in this volume notes this is articulated in the rationalist perspective of IP so long in ascendance. The reason for IP rights has been tied to creating an incentive to innovate. So is it important to have protections for faculty IP and allow them the option to then move their IP into the public domain? Would full openness be a disincentive to some faculty? Could changes to systems that protect faculty IP such as the current tenure system degrade faculty professionalization?

The pressure to commodify faculty scholarship, which in the past often ended up in the public realm, means that far less of the IP of faculty is being shared in ways to support the public good. Many campus IP policies suggest that bringing innovations to market is in the interest of the public good and that their policies on IP actually expedite scholarly work contributions to the public realm. However, changes in the research process also include what faculty do with their research results. Within a traditional academic culture, faculty reputation has been largely based on being the first to publish research results in scholarly journals in the public domain. By participating in the patent process, faculty instead engage in the restriction of the public domain. Further, the insertion of the university technology transfer office and corporate funders into the research process delays publication during the patent application process, which may include prior corporate review to determine a corporate funder's interest in covering patent application costs or in anticipated licensing rights.

Faculty academic freedom and rights are important for maintaining high-quality work and scholarship. Thus, faculty autonomy and independence are necessary elements for ensuring work of high quality and integrity that deserves the public trust. Faculty may compromise academic freedom and autonomy as they form partnerships with industry and corporations and as institutional interests in patents and licenses take precedence over public sharing. Academic freedom has given individual faculty control over their research agendas, enabling them to pursue research regardless of the benefits or disadvantages to private or governmental interests.

New Directions for Higher Education • DOI: 10.1002/he

Most of the debate about IP rights is focused on either the faculty members' rights to own their IP or the institutions' rights over faculty IP, but there is very little discussion of the public within these debates at all. Perhaps the most important discussion that needs to happen right now is what is in the public's interest. What evidence can be offered beyond rhetorical arguments about the public good?

Conclusion

In this chapter, I have argued that the issue of faculty IP requires collective action for faculty to regain their rights in an environment of academic capitalism and administrative overreach and complex external partnerships. The good news is that various national organizations and groups are creating needed resources to help these efforts. A collective faculty voice can combat these growing forces, and balance the interests of all parties. Additionally, there is no clear direction that supports the larger public good and we need—as responsible institutional agents—to better understand that issue.

References

Loggie, K. A., Barron, A. E., Gulitz, E., Hohfeld, T. N., Kromrey, J. D., & Sweeney, P. (2007). Intellectual property and online courses. *Quarterly Review of Distance Education, 8*(2), 109–125.

McSherry, C. (2001). *Who owns academic work?* Cambridge, MA: Harvard University Press.

Packard, A. (2002). Copyright or copy wrong: An analysis of university claims to faculty work. *Communication Law & Policy, 7*(3), 275–316.

Smith, M. F., Dougherty, K. A., & Rhoades, G. (2011). Negotiating virtual space. *NEA 2011 Almanac of Higher Education,* 53–70.

ADRIANNA KEZAR *is professor of higher education at the University of Southern California's Rossier School of Education. Her scholarship focuses on change, leadership, governance, and the changing role of faculty.*

INDEX

NEW DIRECTIONS FOR HIGHER EDUCATION

ORDER FORM SUBSCRIPTION AND SINGLE ISSUES

DISCOUNTED BACK ISSUES:

Use this form to receive 20% off all back issues of *New Directions for Higher Education.*
All single issues priced at **$23.20** (normally $29.00)

TITLE	ISSUE NO.	ISBN
_____	_____	_____
_____	_____	_____
_____	_____	_____

Call 1-800-835-6770 or see mailing instructions below. When calling, mention the promotional code JBNND to receive your discount. For a complete list of issues, please visit www.wiley.com/WileyCDA/WileyTitle/productCd-HE.html

SUBSCRIPTIONS: (1 YEAR, 4 ISSUES)

☐ New Order   ☐ Renewal

U.S.	☐ Individual: $89	☐ Institutional: $356
CANADA/MEXICO	☐ Individual: $89	☐ Institutional: $398
ALL OTHERS	☐ Individual: $113	☐ Institutional: $434

Call 1-800-835-6770 or see mailing and pricing instructions below.
Online subscriptions are available at www.onlinelibrary.wiley.com

ORDER TOTALS:

Issue / Subscription Amount: $ _____

Shipping Amount: $ _____
(for single issues only – subscription prices include shipping)

Total Amount: $ _____

SHIPPING CHARGES:

First Item $6.00
Each Add'l Item $2.00

(No sales tax for U.S. subscriptions. Canadian residents, add GST for subscription orders. Individual rate subscriptions must be paid by personal check or credit card. Individual rate subscriptions may not be resold as library copies.)

BILLING & SHIPPING INFORMATION:

☐ **PAYMENT ENCLOSED:** *(U.S. check or money order only. All payments must be in U.S. dollars.)*

☐ **CREDIT CARD:**   ☐ VISA   ☐ MC   ☐ AMEX

Card number _____ Exp. Date _____

Card Holder Name_____ Card Issue # _____

Signature _____ Day Phone_____

☐ **BILL ME:** *(U.S. institutional orders only. Purchase order required.)*

Purchase order # _____
                     Federal Tax ID 13559302 • GST 89102-8052

Name_____

Address_____

Phone_____ E-mail_____

Copy or detach page and send to: **John Wiley & Sons, Inc. / Jossey Bass**
                                     PO Box 55381
                                     Boston, MA 02205-9850

PROMO JBNND

SAY HELLO TO YOUR INCOMING CLASS
THEY'RE NOT MILLENLIALS ANYMORE

"[A] groundbreaking study [that] provides leaders at all levels the understanding of today's student that is critical to creating the conditions that help students thrive."
— **DR. KEITH HUMPHREY**, vice president for student a airs, and past president, ACPA–College Student Educators International

"Already, it has accelerated my getting acquainted with Generation Z in our work on college campuses. The data is first, fresh and insightful."
— **DR. TIM ELMORE**, president, GrowingLeaders.com

"[A] refreshing, straight-forward and optimistic portrayal of today's college student [that] will change how educators develop, empower and relate to them."
— **NANCY HUNTER DENNEY**, executive director, Lead365 National Conference

COREY SEEMILLER
MEGHAN GRACE

GENERATION Z GOES TO COLLEGE

B JOSSEY-BASS™
A Wiley Brand

❝ Timely and relevant... the book is a must-read for any college student educator! **❞**
— **DR. PAIGE HABER-CURRAN**, assistant professor, Texas State University

Generation Z is rapidly replacing Millennials on college campuses. Those born 1995–2010 have different motivations, learning styles, characteristics, skill sets, and social concerns than previous generations. Unlike Millennials, these students grew up in a recession and are under few illusions. *Generation Z Goes to College* is the first book on how this up-and-coming generation will change higher education, reporting findings from an in-depth study of over 1,100 college students from 15 vastly different higher education institutions.

FIND OUT WHAT YOUR NEXT INCOMING CLASS IS ALL ABOUT.

B JOSSEY-BASS
A Wiley Brand